Valiante

WHAT YOUR SECOND GRADER NEEDS TO KNOW

THE
CORE KNOWLEDGE
SERIES

RESOURCE BOOKS FOR
GRADES ONE THROUGH SIX
BOOK II

Delta
Trade Paperbacks

THE·CORE·KNOWLEDGE
SERIES

WHAT YOUR SECOND GRADER NEEDS TO KNOW

FUNDAMENTALS OF A GOOD SECOND-GRADE EDUCATION

Edited by

E. D. HIRSCH, JR.

A Delta Book
Published by
Dell Publishing
a division of
Bantam Doubleday Dell Publishing Group, Inc.
1540 Broadway
New York, New York 10036

ISBN: 0-385-31027-7

Reprinted by arrangement with Doubleday, a division of Bantam Doubleday Dell Publishing Group, Inc.

Manufactured in the United States of America

Published simultaneously in Canada

August 1993

10   9   8   7   6   5   4

RRH

This book is dedicated to those whose vision and courage have made them pioneers in putting core knowledge into practice:

Constance Jones, Principal,
the Three Oaks Elementary School,
Lee County, Florida

J. P. Lutz,
Director of Elementary Education,
Lee County, Florida

The entire staff of
the Three Oaks Elementary School

"Nothing happens unless first a dream"
(Carl Sandburg,
Washington Monument by Night)

Acknowledgments

This series has depended upon the help, advice, and encouragement of some two thousand people. Some of those singled out here know already the depth of my gratitude; others may be surprised to find themselves thanked publicly for help they gave quietly and freely for the sake of the enterprise alone. To helpers named and unnamed I am deeply grateful.

Project Manager: Tricia Emlet

Editors: Tricia Emlet (Text), Rae Grant (Art)

Artists and Writers: Nancy Bryson (Physical Sciences), Tricia Emlet (Sayings), Leslie Evans (Artwork), Jonathan Fuqua (Artwork), Julie C. Grant (Artwork), Marie Hawthorne (Science Biographies), John Hirsch (Mathematics), Pamela C. Johnson (History and Geography), Blair Logwood Jones (Literature), Gail Macintosh (Artwork), Elaine Moran (Fine Arts), A. Brooke Russell (Life Sciences), Peter Ryan (Fine Arts & Mythology), Lindley Shutz (Language and Literature), Giuseppe Trogu (Artwork)

Art and Photo Research: Rae Grant

Research Assistants: Martha Clay (Permissions), Elaine Moran (Text), Paige Turner (Text)

Advisers on Multiculturalism: Minerva Allen, Frank de Varona, Mick Fedullo, Dorothy Fields, Elizabeth Fox-Genovese, Marcia Galli, Dan Garner, Henry Louis Gates, Cheryl Kulas, Joseph C. Miller, Gerry Raining Bird, Dorothy Small, Sharon Stewart-Peregoy, Sterling Stuckey, Marlene Walking Bear, Lucille Watahomigie, Ramona Wilson

Advisers on Elementary Education: Joseph Adelson, Isobel Beck, Paul Bell, Carl Bereiter, David Bjorklund, Constance Jones, Elizabeth LaFuze, J. P. Lutz, Jean Osborne, Sandra Scarr, Nancy Stein, Phyllis Wilkin

Advisers on Technical Subject Matters: Richard Anderson, Andrew Gleason, Joseph Kett, Ralph Smith, Nancy Summers, James Trefil

Conferees, March 1990: Nola Bacci, Joan Baratz-Snowden, Thomasyne Beverley, Thomas Blackton, Angela Burkhalter, Monty Caldwell, Thomas M. Carroll, Laura Chapman, Carol Anne Collins, Lou Corsaro, Anne Coughlin, Henry Cotton, Arletta Dimberg, Debra P. Douglas, Patricia Edwards, Janet Elenbogen, Mick Fedullo, Michele Fomalont,

Nancy Gercke, Mamon Gibson, Jean Haines, Barbara Hayes, Stephen Herzog, Helen Kelley, Brenda King, John King, Elizabeth LaFuze, Diana Lam, Nancy Lambert, Doris Langaster, Richard LaPointe, Lloyd Leverton, Madeleine Long, Allen Luster, Joseph McGeehan, Janet McLin, Gloria McPhee, Marcia Mallard, Judith Matz, William J. Moloney, John Morabito, Robert Morrill, Roberta Morse, Karen Nathan, Dawn Nichols, Valeta Paige, Mary Perrin, Joseph Piazza, Jeanne Price, Marilyn Rauth, Judith Raybern, Mary Reese, Richard Rice, Wallace Saval, John Saxon, Jan Schwab, Ted Sharp, Diana Smith, Richard Smith, Trevanian Smith, Carol Stevens, Nancy Summers, Michael Terry, Robert Todd, Elois Veltman, Sharon Walker, Mary Ann Ward, Penny Williams, Charles Wootten, Clarke Worthington, Jane York

The Three Oaks Elementary School: Constance Jones, Principal; Cecelia Cook, Assistant Principal

Teachers: Joanne Anderson, Linda Anderson, Nancy Annichiarico, Deborah Backes, Katherine Ann Bedingfield, Barbara Bittner, Michael Blue, Coral Boudin, Nancy Bulgerin, Jodene Cebak, Cheryl Chastain, Paula Clark, Betty Cook, Laura DeProfio, Holly DeSantis, Cindy Donmoyer, Lisa Eastridge, Amy Germer, Elizabeth Graves, Jennifer Gunder, Eileen Hafer, Helen Hallman, Donna Hernandez, Kathleen Holzborn, Robert Horner, Jenni Jones, Zoe Ann Klusacek, Annette Lopez, Barbara Lyon, Cindy Miller, Lelar Miller, Laura Morse, Karen Naylor, Joanne O'Neill, Jill Pearson, Linda Peck, Rebecca Poppe, Janet Posch, Judy Quest, Angie Richards, Angie Ryan, April Santarelli, Patricia Scott, Patricia Stapleton, Pamela Stewart, Jeanne Storm, Phillip Storm, Katherine Twomey, Karen Ward

Benefactors: the Brown Foundation, the Dade County School District, the Exxon Education Foundation, the Lee County School District, the National Endowment for the Humanities, the Shutz Foundation

Morale Boosters: Polly Hirsch, Robert Payton, Rafe Sagalyn, Nancy Brown Wellin

I extend my warm thanks to all these persons and organizations. I hope that my gratitude to them will in time be complemented by that of parents, teachers, and children. Our grateful acknowledgment to these persons does not imply that we have taken their (sometimes conflicting) advice in every case, or that each of them endorses all aspects of this project. Responsibility for final decisions must rest with the editor alone. Suggestions for improvements are very welcome, and I wish to thank in advance those who send advice for revising and improving this series.

Contents

II. GEOGRAPHY, WORLD CIVILIZATION, AND AMERICAN CIVILIZATION

III. FINE ARTS

V. NATURAL SCIENCES

General Introduction

I. IS YOUR SCHOOL TEACHING A CORE OF KNOWLEDGE?

I recently received a letter from a parent of identical twins. She wrote to express her dismay that her children, who are in the same grade in the same school, are learning completely different things. How can this be? It can be because they are in different classrooms; because the teachers in these classrooms have only the vaguest guidelines to follow; in short, because the school, like most in the United States, lacks a definite, specific curriculum.

Many parents would be surprised if they were to examine the curriculum of their child's elementary school. I urge you to ask to see your school's curriculum. Does it say just what specific core of content each child at a particular grade level is expected to learn by the end of the year? That is highly unlikely since most curricula speak in vague terms of general skills, processes, and attitudes. This vagueness is no virtue. It places unreasonable demands upon teachers and often results in years of schooling marred by repetitions and gaps: yet another unit on dinosaurs; *Charlotte's Web* for the third time. "You've never heard of the Bill of Rights?" "You've never been taught how to add two fractions with unlike denominators?"

When identical twins in two classrooms of the same school have no academic experiences in common, that is a sign of trouble. When teachers in that school do not know what children in other classrooms are learning on the same grade level, much less in earlier and later grades, they cannot reliably predict that children will be prepared with a shared core of knowledge and skills. The result of this curricular incoherence is that many schools fall far short of developing the full potentials of our children.

To address this problem, I started the Core Knowledge Foundation in 1986. This book and its companion volumes in the *Core Knowledge Series* are designed to give parents, teachers, and, through them, children a carefully sequenced body of knowledge that we call core knowledge.

Core knowledge is, first of all, a body of widely used knowledge taken for granted by competent writers and speakers in the United States. Because this knowledge is taken for granted rather than explained when it is used, it forms a necessary foundation for the higher-order reading, writing, and thinking skills that children need for academic and vocational success. The universal attainment of such knowledge should be a central aim of curricula in our elementary schools, just as it is currently the aim in all world-class educational systems.

For reasons explained in the next section, making sure that all young children in the United States possess a core of shared knowledge is a necessary step in developing a first-rate educational system.

II. WHY CORE KNOWLEDGE IS NEEDED

Learning builds on learning. Children (and adults) gain new knowledge only by building on what they already know. It is essential to begin building solid foundations of knowledge in the early grades, when children are most receptive, because research has shown that for the vast majority of children, academic deficiencies from the first six grades *permanently* impair the success of later learning. Poor performance of American students in middle and high schools may be traced directly to shortcomings inherited from elementary schools that have not imparted to children the knowledge they need for further learning.

All of the highest-achieving and most egalitarian elementary school systems in the world (such as those in Sweden, France, and Japan) teach a specific core of knowledge in each of the first six grades, thus enabling all their children to enter each new grade with a secure foundation for further learning. It is time American schools did so as well, for the following reasons:

1. *Commonly shared knowledge makes schooling more effective.* We know that the one-on-one tutorial is the most effective form of schooling, in part because a parent or teacher can provide tailor-made instruction for the individual child. But in a nontutorial situation—in, for example, a typical classroom with twenty-five or more students—the instructor cannot effectively impart new knowledge to all the students unless each one shares the background knowledge that the lesson is being built upon. When all the students in a class *do* share that relevant background knowledge, a classroom can begin to approach the effectiveness of a tutorial. Even when some children in a class don't have elements of the core knowledge they were supposed to acquire in previous grades, the existence of a specifically defined core makes it possible for the teacher or parent to identify and fill the gaps, thus giving all students a chance to fulfill their potentials in later grades.

2. *Commonly shared knowledge makes schooling more fair and democratic.* When all the children who enter a grade can be assumed to share some of the same building blocks of knowledge, and when the teacher knows exactly what those building blocks are, then all the students are empowered to learn. In our current system, disadvantaged

children too often suffer from unmerited low expectations that translate into watered-down curricula. But if we specify the core of knowledge that all children should share, then we can guarantee equal access to that knowledge and compensate for the academic advantages some students are offered at home. In a core knowledge school, disadvantaged children, like *all* children, enjoy the benefits of important, challenging knowledge that will provide the foundation for successful later learning.

3. *Commonly shared knowledge helps create cooperation and solidarity in our schools and nation.* Diversity is a hallmark and strength of our nation. American classrooms are usually made up of students from a variety of cultural backgrounds, and those different cultures should be honored and understood by all students as part of the common core. Education should create a *school-based* culture that is common and welcoming to all because it includes knowledge of many cultures and gives all students, no matter what their backgrounds, a common foundation for understanding our cultural diversity.

In the next section I will describe the steps taken by the Core Knowledge Foundation to develop a model of the commonly shared knowledge our children need (which forms the basis for this series of books).

III. THE CONSENSUS BEHIND THE CORE KNOWLEDGE SEQUENCE

The content in this and other volumes in the *Core Knowledge Series* is based on a document called the Core Knowledge Sequence, a grade-by-grade sequence of specific content guidelines in history, geography, mathematics, science, language arts, and the fine arts. The Sequence is not meant to outline the whole of the school curriculum; rather, it offers specific guidelines to knowledge that can reasonably be expected to make up about *half* of any school's curriculum, thus leaving ample room for local requirements and emphases. Teaching a common core of knowledge, such as that articulated in the Core Knowledge Sequence, is compatible with a variety of instructional methods and additional subject matters.

The Core Knowledge Sequence is the result of a long process of research and consensus building undertaken by the nonprofit Core Knowledge Foundation. Here is how we achieved the consensus behind the Core Knowledge Sequence.

First we analyzed the many reports issued by state departments of education and by professional organizations—such as the National Council of Teachers of Mathematics and the American Association for the Advancement of Science—which recommend general outcomes for elementary and secondary education. We also tabulated the knowledge and skills through grade six specified in the successful educational systems of several other countries, including France, Japan, Sweden, and Germany.

In addition, we formed an advisory board on multiculturalism that proposed a core knowledge of diverse cultural traditions that all American children should share as part of their school-based common culture. We sent the resulting materials to three independent groups of teachers, scholars, and scientists around the country and asked them to create a master list of the core knowledge children should have by the end of grade six. About 150 educators (including college professors, scientists, and administrators) were involved in this initial step.

These items were amalgamated into a master plan, and other groups of teachers and specialists were asked to agree on a grade-by-grade sequence of the items. That sequence was then sent to some one hundred educators and specialists who participated in a national conference that was called to hammer out a working agreement on core knowledge for the first six grades.

This important meeting took place in March 1990. The conferees were elementary school teachers, curriculum specialists, scientists, science writers, officers of national organizations, representatives of ethnic groups, district superintendents, and school principals from across the country. A total of twenty-four working groups decided on revisions in the Sequence. The resulting provisional Sequence was further fine-tuned during a year of implementation at a pioneering school, Three Oaks Elementary, in Lee County, Florida. The result is the Core Knowledge Sequence that forms the basis for this series.

IV. THE NATURE OF THIS SERIES

The books in this series are designed to be useful tools for parents and teachers, both at home and in school. They are called resources to signal that they do not replace the regular local school curriculum but rather serve as aids to help children gain some of the important knowledge they will need to make progress in school and be effective in society.

Each book in the *Core Knowledge Series* presents knowledge upon which later books will build. Our writers have tried their best to make the content interesting, clear, and challenging. We have *not* used discredited grade-level formulas regarding vocabulary and sentence length. Drafts of some materials have been revised on the basis of teachers' experiences with children.

Although we have made these books as accessible and useful as we can, parents and teachers should understand that they are not the only means by which the Core

Knowledge Sequence can be imparted. The books represent a single version of the possibilities inherent in the Core Knowledge Sequence and a first step in the core knowledge reform effort. We hope that publishers will be stimulated to offer educational videos, computer software, games, alternative books, and other imaginative vehicles based on the Core Knowledge Sequence.

The Core Knowledge Sequence may be ordered from the Core Knowledge Foundation (please see the end of this introduction for the address).

V. WHAT YOU CAN DO TO HELP IMPROVE AMERICAN EDUCATION

The first step for parents and teachers who are committed to reform is to be skeptical about oversimplified slogans like "Critical thinking" and "Learning to learn." Such slogans are everywhere, and unfortunately for our schools, their partial insights have been elevated to the level of universal truths. For example, "What students learn is not important; rather, we must teach students to learn *how* to learn"; "The child, not the academic subject, is the true focus of education"; "Do not impose knowledge on children before they are developmentally ready to receive it"; "Do not bog children down in mere facts, but rather, inculcate critical-thinking skills."

Who has not heard these sentiments, so admirable and humane and—up to a point—so true? But these positive sentiments in favor of skills and understanding have been turned into negative sentiments against the teaching of important knowledge. Those who have entered the teaching profession over the past forty years have been taught to scorn important knowledge as "mere facts" and to see the imparting of this knowledge as somehow injurious to children. Thus it has come about that many educators, armed with partially true slogans, have seemingly taken leave of common sense.

Many parents and teachers have come to the conclusion that elementary education must strike a better balance between the development of the whole child and the more limited but fundamental duty of the school to ensure that all children master a core of knowledge essential to their competence as learners in later grades. But these parents and teachers cannot act on their convictions without access to an agreed-upon concrete sequence of knowledge. Our main motivation in developing the Core Knowledge Sequence and this book series has been to give parents and teachers something concrete to work with.

It has been encouraging to see how many teachers, since the first volume in this series was published, have responded to the core knowledge reform effort. A small but growing number of schools around the country—more than fifty as of this writing, in diverse regions serving diverse populations—are working to integrate core knowledge into their curricula.

Parents and teachers are urged to join in a grass-roots effort to strengthen our elementary schools. The place to start is your own school and district. Insist that your school clearly state the core of *specific* knowledge that each child in a grade must learn. Whether your school's core corresponds to the core knowledge model is less important than the existence of *some* core, which, we hope, will be as solid, coherent, and challenging as core knowledge has proved to be. Inform members of your community about the need for such a specific curriculum, and help make sure that the people who are elected or appointed to your local school board are independent-minded people who will insist that our children have the benefit of a solid, specific, world-class curriculum in each grade.

You are invited to become a member of the Core Knowledge Network by writing the Core Knowledge Foundation, 2012-B Morton Drive, Charlottesville, VA 22901.

Share the knowledge!

E. D. Hirsch, Jr.
Charlottesville, Virginia

How to Use This Book

1. Reading and Listening as an Active Adventure

A wonderful way for a child to learn is to interact with some-one who is reading aloud. Active, engaged learning is remembered better than passive learning. Many adults, when reading aloud, instinctively draw children into the story by asking them questions that help children to learn for themselves and to connect the narrative with their own experience. All subject matters are appropriate for this interactive mode of reading aloud to children. Take for example the following passage from the section on "Physical Sciences":

"Some say that the greatest scientist who ever lived was a physicist. He was Isaac Newton, an Englishman who lived over three hundred years ago. The story goes that young Isaac became fascinated with what makes things move when he looked out his bedroom window and spied an apple falling from a tree in the yard. 'Why do things fall down?' he asked himself. 'Why don't they go sideways, or some other direction?' When he grew up he answered that question and many others as well."

READER: Why do things fall down, Carla?

CHILD: Because they're heavy?

READER: Right! But why do heavy things fall down instead of up or sideways? That's what Newton wanted to know.

CHILD: I don't know. Because everything falls down?

READER: Let's look at the globe of the earth. Think of people on the other side of the world in Australia, say. Do things fall down for those people too?

CHILD: I guess so.

READER: That's right, they do. But you can see that down for them is up for us.

CHILD: Show me.

READER: When you look at the globe you see that down really means toward the middle of the earth. So down for them is up for us, but down is always toward the center of the earth.

CHILD: Okay.

READER: Newton guessed that all things pull at each other, and the heavier a thing is the harder it pulls. What's the heaviest thing on earth?

CHILD: A skyscraper!

READER: That's very heavy. But isn't the whole earth the heaviest thing of all?

CHILD: Yes.

READER: The earth is the heaviest thing. Newton figured out that everything is pulled toward the center of the earth, which is always straight down from where we are. That's why everything falls down.

Depending on the child's interest, the subject could be taken further. A particular advantage of interactive reading is its potential to stimulate a child's curiosity and further learning by using actual objects and experiences. Such "hands-on" activities and discussions are thought to be the best way to learn about science—and other subjects, too. Of course, many children will be much more interested in discussing why "Beauty" was so nice to "Beast" than in considering why things fall down. A sensitive parent or teacher will know how to engage the particular interest and curiosity of individual children.

The writers of this book have tried to encourage children to interact with what they read here. But nothing can replace the active participation of adults as they help children enter into the vivid meaning of what is read.

2. Repetition

Do not hesitate to read sections aloud more than once. Young children like to hear good stories over and over again. The joy children take from repetition comes partly from the pleasure all people take in what is familiar and expected, but it also comes from their pleasure in fulfilling an instinct to learn securely, and truly to *possess* knowledge.

More advice to parents and teachers about teaching the specific subject matter is provided in the introduction to each section.

Joyful reading!

I.

LANGUAGE ARTS

Introduction to Stories and Poems

FOR PARENTS AND TEACHERS

Under "stories," we have included narrative poems by Clement Clark Moore and Henry Wadsworth Longfellow, as well as narratives that are more demanding than those for grade one. Two of the stories are retellings of tales by Charles Dickens ("A Christmas Carol") and J. M. Barrie ("Peter Pan").

Parents have recently been demanding that our schools once again teach traditional values such as honesty, courage, and diligence. The stories and poems that we tell our children powerfully convey ethical and social values that will later become part of their habitual world.

Some traditional values are universal and are found in many other cultures. The tale from Asia about "One-Inch Fellow" teaches loyalty no less than does "Beauty and the Beast." The value of kindness to strangers comes across in the American Indian tale "Inktomi Lost His Eyes," as well as in Dickens's "A Christmas Carol."

Those parents who hope that schooling will instill ethical values can feel somewhat reassured if their children are being taught good literature. For, next to human role models who actually exemplify patience, courage, tolerance, and civility (such role models are of course the best teachers of virtue), literature must be counted as one of the better nurturers of ethical and social values. The great philosopher Plato said that stories are the most important part of early education, and advised parents and teachers to take great care in choosing the right stories. "Let them fashion the mind with such tales even more fondly than they mold the body."

As memorably as anyone before or since, Philip Sidney depicted the poet and storyteller as a teacher of values to mankind:

With a tale forsooth he cometh unto you, with a tale which holdeth children from play, and old men from the chimney corner. And pretending no more, doth intend the winning of the mind from wickedness to virtue: even as the child is often brought to take most wholesome things by hiding them in such other as have a pleasant taste.

STORIES AND POEMS

Beauty and the Beast

There was once a wealthy merchant who lost all of his ships at sea. He and his three daughters had to move to a cottage in the woods. One day, the merchant heard that one of his ships had landed with its cargo safe. He joyfully prepared to fetch his goods, asking each of his daughters what he might bring her. The older two asked for gowns and jewels, but the youngest, who was called Beauty, asked only for a single rose.

When the merchant reached the ship, he found that his goods had been stolen. Disappointed, he turned for home, wondering how to tell his daughters. As he rode along, suddenly he came upon a palace with lights blazing. The tired merchant entered the wide-open door and found a fine dinner laid out just for him. When he had eaten, he began to look for his mysterious host in order to thank him. He found a beautiful garden, blooming in the midst of winter. There amid all the bright blossoms was a gorgeous rosebush. He plucked a single rose.

"How dare you!" snarled a voice. The startled merchant turned around to see a creature, half-man and half-beast.

"Please," said the frightened man, "I only wanted it for my daughter, Beauty."

"For plucking that rose you must pay a price," said the Beast. "Either send your daughter Beauty to me, or prepare to lose your life!" The sad father returned home and told Beauty what had happened. When Beauty heard of

the Beast's terrible command, she was frightened. But to save her father she went to the Beast, leaving her father and sisters to wait and hope for her return.

The Beast treated Beauty with great kindness. Though she spent her days alone, the birds sang to her and kept her company, and the lovely gardens of the palace made her heart glad. Every evening as she sat down to a fine supper, the Beast appeared to talk with her as she ate. Although his looks frightened her at first, she soon grew used to them, for he was in every other way a considerate friend. Soon she looked forward to their meetings. When the meal was over and it was time to say good night, the Beast would ask her, "Do you love me?" But as much as she cared for him, Beauty always had to answer, "No."

After a time, the Beast told Beauty that she could visit her family. He bade her good-bye sadly, for he feared that she would never return. He gave her a magic ring. "If ever you wish to return to me," he said, "you only have to turn the stone and say, 'I want to go back to my Beast.' " Then he gave her rich gifts for her father and sisters, and sent her home on his magic horse.

Beauty's father and sisters were overjoyed to see her. They thought of many reasons to make her visit last longer. Finally one night, Beauty awoke from a dream that the Beast was dying. "I must go to him!" she cried. She turned the ring, and found herself in the Beast's garden, near the beautiful rosebush. There on the ground lay the Beast, dying for sorrow that Beauty was gone. "I have returned!" she said. The Beast looked up and said in a weak voice, "Is it true then? Do you love me, Beauty?" "Yes, yes!" she cried. Suddenly the Beast changed before her eyes into a strong and handsome prince, for Beauty's love had freed him from a wicked curse. The two were married with her father's blessing, and they lived happily ever after.

The Blind Men and the Elephant

There were once six blind men who went to see an elephant. The first blind man stretched his hands in front of him and felt the animal's huge side. "This elephant is like a high, strong wall," he announced.

The second man, who was standing near the elephant's head, put his hand on its long, sharp tusk. "A wall? No! I would say that it is more like a spear."

The third man reached around the elephant's leg with both arms. "I hate to contradict you," he said, "but I am sure that the elephant is very like a tree."

The fourth man happened to reach up and touch the elephant's ear. "All of you are mistaken," he said. "The elephant is actually similar to a fan."

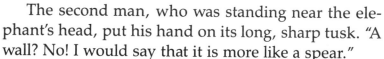

The fifth man was standing by himself at the elephant's other end. He happened to grab the animal's tail. "I don't understand the confusion," he said. "I am sure I am correct in saying that the elephant is much like a rope."

Now the elephant was a bit playful, so he tickled the sixth man with his trunk. The startled man pushed the trunk away and said with a shudder, "Please stay calm while I swear to you that the elephant is really a very large snake!"

"Nonsense!" said the others. Still, they quietly began to move away, and they never bothered to put their heads together to understand what the elephant was really like.

A Christmas Carol

Old Ebenezer Scrooge sat in his counting house on Christmas Eve. His poor clerk, Bob Cratchit, shivered as he worked in the next room, for Scrooge gave him scarcely one coal for his fire.

"I suppose you'll be wanting tomorrow off," Scrooge said gruffly to his clerk as the day ended. "Well, mind that you be here early the next morning."

"Thank you, sir," said Bob, wrapping himself in the blanket that served for his coat, "and Merry Christmas to you, sir."

Scrooge snapped, "Bah! Humbug!" Then he closed the office and went home alone.

As he approached his front door, Scrooge blinked his eyes. Was that a face on the knocker? Yes—the face of his former partner, now dead, Jacob Marley!

The face vanished as suddenly as it had appeared. But when Scrooge had closed himself in his room, he was startled by the sound of clanking chains. Right through the closed door of his room walked the ghost of Jacob Marley. His arms and legs were wrapped in a long chain, from which hung many locked boxes of money. "I wear the chain I forged in life," said the ghost to the frightened Scrooge. "You are making your own chain now, Ebenezer, for you care too much for the business of making money and too little for the business of your fellow man! You must change before it is too late." The ghost told Scrooge that he would be visited by three spirits. Then he vanished.

As the clock struck one, the curtains of Scrooge's bed were pulled aside by the first spirit, who looked like a child with long, white hair, holding a sprig of holly in his hand. From the top of his head shone a bright light. "I am the Ghost of Christmas Past," he said. He took Scrooge by the hand and led him out the window, flying through the night air. They came to rest at a boarding school. The children were gone, for it was Christmastime. Among all the empty desks sat one lone boy, reading. His friends and family had not invited him home for Christmas. "Why, that's me!" said Scrooge. As he recalled his sad childhood, he began to weep.

Scrooge was next visited by a huge, jolly spirit who wore a bright robe and a garland of fruit on his head. This was the Ghost of Christmas Present. He showed Scrooge a vision of happy people everywhere, wishing one another good cheer and making ready for the Christmas celebration. Then he showed him the home of Bob Cratchit, where the family was sitting down to a meager Christmas dinner. To Scrooge's surprise, they seemed as happy as if they had a great feast before them. Happiest of all was the youngest child, a frail boy named Tiny Tim, who walked with a crutch. Bob Cratchit said, "A Merry Christmas to us all, my dears. God bless us!" And Tiny Tim answered sweetly, "God bless us, every one!" Scrooge was touched to see how Bob held his little boy close by his side, as if he were afraid of losing him. "Spirit," said Scrooge, "tell me if Tiny Tim will live."

"If these shadows remain unchanged by the future," said the ghost, "the child will die." Scrooge was filled with sorrow. The ghost of Christmas Present disappeared. Then Scrooge looked up and saw a solemn phantom, draped and hooded. Though it said nothing, Scrooge knew that it must be the Ghost of Christmas Yet to Come. The phantom took Scrooge back to the home of Bob Cratchit, where all was now quiet and solemn. In the corner a crutch leaned against the wall, next to an empty little chair. "Ah, poor Tiny Tim!" thought Scrooge, guessing what had happened. The other family members consoled one another. "I am sure we shall none of us forget poor Tiny Tim, shall we?" said his father. "Never!" they cried. As he watched, Scrooge's heart reached out to them.

Now the hooded figure showed Scrooge a different house, where a dead man lay on a bed, his face and body covered by a sheet. Outside, people joked about the dead man, glad to be rid of him. "Specter," said Scrooge, "tell me what man that was whom we saw lying dead." The ghost silently led him to a churchyard, and pointed to the name written upon a grave stone.

It read EBENEZER SCROOGE. "Oh no, no!" cried Scrooge. "Good spirit, tell me that I may change these shadows you have shown me, by changing my life!" But the ghost said nothing. As the light of morning brightened the room, Scrooge realized he had been staring at a bedpost.

Only a bedpost! When Scrooge discovered that he was alive and in his own bed, and that Christmas morning was only just beginning, he leaped up with joy and vowed to change his life. He would share his wealth. He would help others. He rushed out to buy the biggest turkey in town, and he sent it to Bob Cratchit's house.

The next day, he gave Bob Cratchit a raise. And to Tiny Tim, who did *not* die, he became a second father from that time on. He became as good a friend, as good a master, and as good a man as the city knew; and it was always said of him that he knew how to keep Christmas well. May such good things be truly said of all of us! And so, as Tiny Tim observed, "God bless us, every one!"

El Pajaro Cu

When God made the world, he took great care in forming the birds. He made their bodies and then feathered them, creating owl and dove and peacock, each different from the other. And then he ran out of feathers. The last bird, Pajaro Cu, received no feathers whatsoever. Pajaro Cu didn't seem to care. He went anywhere he wished, never caring that he was as naked as the palm of your hand.

But the other birds worried.

"What can we do for him?" asked Owl.

"Pity on the little thing," said Dove.

"He looks awful," said Peacock.

"All of the other animals talk about him."

The birds agreed that something must be done.

Then Owl said, "If we each give him one of our feathers, he'll be completely covered, and we'll never feel the difference."

All of the birds thought this was a splendid idea. Parrot gave a green feather; Canary's was yellow; Guinea Bird offered silver; Crow gave black; Swan's was white; and Redbird gave a bright red feather. Just as Pajaro Cu was about to receive his new coat, Peacock suddenly screeched, "No! With these feathers, Pajaro Cu will be the most beautiful bird around, and before long, he will be strutting about with pride."

"But we can't leave him naked," said Dove. "He is a disgrace to the entire community of birds!"

Everyone, including Pajaro Cu, wondered what to do.

"I know," said Owl. "If you each give him your feather, I will watch over him and protect us all from his vanity."

In no time at all, Pajaro Cu was the best-dressed bird around. Even Peacock was awed into silence. Lifting his glistening wings, Pajaro Cu flew straight to the pond, where he took one look at his marvelous self, and darted high up toward heaven.

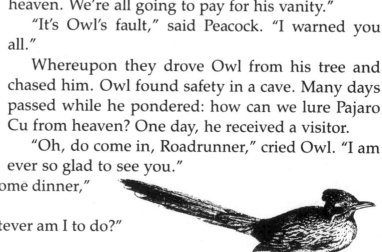

Owl, old and heavy, tried to follow him, but his short wings weren't meant for such flying. Slowly, he spiraled back down to earth, where he found the others waiting in the branches.

Parrot said, "None of us has ever flown to heaven. We're all going to pay for his vanity."

"It's Owl's fault," said Peacock. "I warned you all."

Whereupon they drove Owl from his tree and chased him. Owl found safety in a cave. Many days passed while he pondered: how can we lure Pajaro Cu from heaven? One day, he received a visitor.

"Oh, do come in, Roadrunner," cried Owl. "I am ever so glad to see you."

"I have brought you some dinner," Roadrunner said.

"Thank you. But whatever am I to do?" said Owl.

"You must stay here," Roadrunner warned. "Crow has sworn to kill you unless you retrieve his feather."

Owl said, "Then I will hunt by night, when Crow is asleep. And I will call for Pajaro Cu until he comes."

"And I will search for him on the road," said Roadrunner.

Even today they are looking. This is why Roadrunner streaks from one place to another, searching the road for Pajaro Cu. And when you listen at night, you can hear Owl calling, "Cu, Cu, Cu, Cu, Cu."

The Emperor's New Clothes

There was once an Emperor who loved fine clothes. He scarcely let a day pass without parading some gorgeous new outfit before his subjects. One day as his procession made its way through the crowd, he was approached by two crooks. They told him that they were weavers from a far land who had learned the art of making a special cloth that would surpass any he had ever seen before. It was the most beautiful fabric in the world, they said, yet it could be seen only by those who were wise and able.

The Emperor gave them a great sum of money and told them to begin weaving the special cloth right away. Day and night, the two stayed behind the closed door of their weaving room. The Emperor grew curious to see what they were making. But fearing that he might be unable to see the magic cloth, he first sent his chief adviser instead. The adviser entered the room to find the weavers hard at work, their shuttles flying through a completely empty loom. "Do you like it?" they asked. The adviser dared not admit that he could see no cloth at all. People would know that he was a fool! He pretended to like the cloth a great deal, and as the two weavers talked of its colors and its smoothness, he remembered everything so that he might report it to the Emperor.

Now the Emperor went to take a look for himself. After all, if his adviser had seen the cloth, certainly he himself would have no problem. But though the two weavers appeared to be working hard, the Emperor saw nothing at all on their looms. "I must be stupid and incompetent!" he thought. But he pretended to be delighted with the beautiful cloth, and he told the weavers to prepare his new suit of clothes as soon as possible. When they asked him for more money, he gave it to them readily.

At last the day came for the Emperor to wear his new clothes in public. The dishonest weavers had made a great show for days, cutting and sewing their invisible cloth before an open window for all to see. All those who watched pretended to admire the supposedly beautiful cloth, for none wished to be thought stupid or incompetent. The weavers entered the Emperor's dressing chamber holding their arms high, as if to keep the new garments from dragging on the floor. They carefully dressed the Emperor in the make-believe clothes, saying how well they suited him, though the Emperor could plainly see in the mirror that he was stark naked.

The Emperor stepped out of the palace, attended by many advisers, officers, and servants. The people looked on, all pretending to be awed by the beautiful new clothes that his majesty the Emperor was wearing. No one had the courage to speak the truth, until a little child called out loudly, "But he has no clothes on!" At first there was shocked silence. Then, someone began to giggle, then another laughed. Soon all were laughing and saying, "The child has spoken the truth. He isn't wearing a thing!" At last the Emperor understood how he had been fooled, and he marched quickly back into the palace, blushing from head to toe.

Hansel and Gretel

Once there was a poor woodcutter who could barely feed his two children, Hansel and Gretel. One night after the children had gone to bed, their stepmother said, "We shall soon starve if we go on feeding those children of yours! Let us take them into the woods and leave them." Shocked, the father at first refused. But being a coward, he gave in to his wife at last. The boy Hansel overheard his father and his stepmother; so, when they had gone to bed, he sneaked out and filled his pockets with small white pebbles.

The next morning the stepmother told the children, "Come with us to the forest to cut wood." She gave them each a scrap of bread. As they walked along, Hansel lingered behind, secretly dropping his pebbles here and there on the path. When they were deep in the woods, their father built a fire and told them to wait until he returned. The children soon fell asleep.

When they awoke, the fire had gone out, and it was dark. "They have forgotten us!" cried Gretel. Hansel showed her the trail of pebbles, shining in the moonlight, and they followed them home. Their father was overjoyed to see them.

Not long afterward, the stepmother again told the father that they must lose the children in the woods, and again he gave in. When Hansel tried to gather pebbles, this time he found the door locked fast. So the next day, as they set out for the forest, he dropped crumbs from his bread along the trail.

That night, the children awoke as before to find themselves in cold darkness. But when Hansel looked for the trail of crumbs, he found that the birds had eaten every one. All night the frightened children wandered. When the sky at last grew light again, they found themselves in a clearing, where there stood a gingerbread house with sugar-pane windows. They were so hungry that they broke off pieces of the house and began eating. Suddenly a voice said, "Nibble, nibble, like a mouse. Who is nibbling on my house?" They looked up to see an old witch. She grabbed Hansel and threw him in a cage. Then she said to Gretel, "Come, lazybones, you must cook something delicious for your brother. When we have fattened him up, I shall eat him!" Gretel was horrified, but she decided to obey the witch until she could think of a way to save her brother.

Each day the witch went to the bars of Hansel's cage and told him to stick out a finger. Knowing that she could not see well, Hansel thrust a twig through the bars instead. "Still too thin!" she said angrily. Finally the witch said that she could wait no longer. She would eat Hansel, thin or fat. She fired the oven and ordered Gretel to lean in to see if it were hot. Gretel guessed that the witch planned to bake her, too. She whined, "I don't know how to do it. Will you show me?"

"Idiot!" screamed the witch. "I'll do it myself." She opened the oven door and stuck her head in. In a flash, Gretel pushed her in, slammed the door closed, and ran to free Hansel.

The children ran until, by chance, they found themselves back at their own

cottage once more. Their happy father begged their forgiveness and told them that their stepmother was dead. The children embraced him, and from that day forth, they all cared for one another through the most difficult times.

Inktomi Lost His Eyes
(A STORY FROM THE ASSINIBOINE TRIBE)

Inktomi was walking through the woods one afternoon when he heard a strange noise: a bird was singing in his language, Assiniboine! Each time the bird sang the Assiniboine song, its eyes flew from its head and perched in the top of a tall tree, and when it sang another song, its eyes fluttered back again.

Inktomi wanted to learn this trick because he thought everyone would admire his power so much that he could be a great chief someday. He asked, "Little brother, would you please show me how to do that?"

After the bird taught Inktomi how to do the trick, he warned him, "You must use this trick no more than four times."

Inktomi tried it once to make sure it worked. Sure enough, his eyes flew up to the treetop and then fluttered down again. He was so excited that he tried it a second time and a third time. And when he ran into Brother Gopher, he did it again, just to show off. Gopher was very impressed. But Inktomi forgot that he had now used the trick four times.

When he returned to camp, he gathered everyone around to watch his powerful trick. Inktomi sang the bird's song, and up flew his eyes to a treetop. Inktomi was very proud, and the people gasped. He sang again, and waited for the people to praise him. But his eyes refused to come back. Inktomi pleaded with his eyes, and the people began to laugh.

Inktomi was frightened because he had not listened to the bird's warning, and he stumbled from the camp to find the bird. He couldn't see a thing! Suddenly, he heard a little field mouse ask, "Why are you crying?" When Inktomi explained, the little mouse felt sorry for him. "Take one of my eyes," he said, "and then you won't be afraid." Inktomi thanked the little mouse, and set out again.

Soon, he ran into a buffalo calf. "Why are you blinded in one eye?" the calf asked. When Inktomi told him, the calf said, "Take one of my eyes, and then you can find the bird." And Inktomi took one of the calf's eyes and thanked it.

Blessed with the kindness and the sight of the animals, it wasn't long before Inktomi found the bird. "Please help me," he said. "I will never again be so vain or try to be more powerful than anyone else." With this promise, the bird taught him a new song, and when Inktomi sang it, his eyes flew down from the tree and returned to his head. Happy, Inktomi set out to give the animals their own eyes back.

'Twas the Night Before Christmas
BY CLEMENT C. MOORE

'Twas the night before Christmas,
When all through the house
Not a creature was stirring, not even a mouse.
The stockings were hung by the chimney with care,
In hopes that St. Nicholas soon would be there.
The children were nestled all snug in their beds,
While visions of sugar plums danced in their heads.
And mama in her kerchief, and I in my cap
Had just settled down for a long winter's nap,
When out on the lawn there arose such a clatter,
I sprang from my bed to see what was the matter.
Away to the window I flew like a flash,
Tore open the shutters and threw up the sash.
The moon on the breast of the new fallen snow
Gave the luster of midday to objects below.
When what to my wondering eyes should appear,
But a miniature sleigh and eight tiny reindeer
With a little old driver so lively and quick
I knew in a moment it must be St. Nick.
More rapid than eagles his coursers they came,

And he whistled, and shouted, and called them by name:
"Now, Dasher! Now, Dancer! Now, Prancer and Vixen!
On, Comet! On, Cupid! On, Donner and Blitzen!
To the top of the porch! To the top of the wall!
Now dash away! Dash away! Dash away all!"
As dry leaves that before the wild hurricane fly,
When they meet with an obstacle, mount to the sky,
So up to the housetop the coursers they flew,
With a sleigh full of toys, and St. Nicholas, too.
And then, in a twinkling, I heard on the roof
The prancing and pawing of each little hoof.

As I drew in my head, and was turning around . . .
Down the chimney St. Nicholas came with a bound!
He was dressed all in fur from his head to his foot,
And his clothes were all tarnished with ashes and soot;
A bundle of toys he had flung on his back,
And he looked like a peddler just opening his pack.
His eyes—how they twinkled, his dimples how merry!
His cheeks were like roses, his nose like a cherry!
His droll little mouth was drawn up like a bow,
And the beard on his chin was as white as the snow.
The stump of a pipe he held tight in his teeth,
And the smoke it encircled his head like a wreath.
He had a broad face and a round little belly
That shook when he laughed like a bowl full of jelly.
He was chubby and plump, a right jolly old elf,
And I laughed when I saw him in spite of myself!
A wink of his eye and a twist of his head
Soon gave me to know I had nothing to dread.
He spoke not a word, but went straight to his work,
And filled all the stockings—then turned with a jerk . . .
And laying his finger aside of his nose,
And giving a nod, up the chimney he rose!
He sprang to his sleigh, to his team gave a whistle,
And away they all flew like the down of a thistle.
But I heard him exclaim, 'ere he drove out of sight . . .
"Happy Christmas to all, And to all a good night!"

One-Inch Fellow

Long ago, in the Japanese village of Naniwa, there lived an old couple who, more than anything, wanted a child. One night, as they were praying, they saw a cloud drift away from the moon and float slowly toward their home. And the next morning, their wish was granted. When the cloud floated away, it left them with a son. The old couple called him Isun Boshi, the "One-Inch Fellow," for he was no taller than his father's thumb!

Isun Boshi was a loving son, who helped his parents in every way. When his mother lost her sewing needles on the floor, he found them. And at night, he made his parents laugh with tales of hiding from his friends who could never find him. Fourteen years went by and, though he had grown no taller, Isun Boshi wanted to go out into the world.

"Honorable Mother, and Honorable Father," he said, "I would like your permission to go to the capital and make a name for myself."

His parents were worried that he would not be able to protect himself, but they agreed. His mother presented him with a kimono, which she had sewn in bright colors so that no one would step on him. His father gave him a boat, which he had made from a rice bowl. On the morning he was to leave, Isun Boshi picked a chopstick to use as a paddle, and was on his way.

After many days, he sailed into the bustling city of Kyoto. He walked carefully through the streets, dodging feet and cart wheels. The houses were larger than any he had known in Naniwa. On the front steps of the largest house sat a pair of shiny black shoes. Isun Boshi sat down beside them to rest. He didn't know that they belonged to the wealthiest lord in the city.

When a man stepped from the door, Isun Boshi cried, "I'm new here and I'd like to work for you!"

The lord looked all around him.

"Down here!" Isun Boshi cried.

The lord of the shiny black shoes was so surprised to find a person this small that he hired Isun Boshi right away. No one else in Kyoto had a servant who was smaller—or who worked harder.

Isun Boshi also won the attention of the man's daughter, the princess. They paraded through the city together during the New Year celebration, and they traveled together in the spring to the Cherry Blossom Festival. And when fall came, the lord chose Isun Boshi to escort his daughter to the Shrine of Ise. Every woman traveled there at least once before her marriage.

The princess and her escorts had made their way safely to the shrine and were on the way home again, when they began to hear strange noises behind them on the narrow road. They could see nothing in the shadows, when suddenly, a huge monster leaped into their path. Everyone fled or fainted except Isun Boshi and the princess.

"What are you?" Isun Boshi cried.

"I am an Oni," rasped the terrible monster, "and I am going to gobble you up!" With that, he snatched up Isun Boshi and popped him into his mouth. Down Isun Boshi slid. Taking out the sword his mother had made for him from her sewing needle, he poked and prodded the walls of the Oni's stomach. The Oni wheezed and burped and, finally, sneezed, sending Isun Boshi onto the road with a tiny crash. Pin-pricked and angry, the Oni leaped back into the shadows.

The princess picked up the hammer he had dropped. When they were safe, she looked at it more closely.

"Isun Boshi," she said, "that was no Oni. For this is a magic hammer and they are carried only

by the gods! That must have been a god who was sent down to test you! If you strike the hammer, you may have whatever you wish."

Isun Boshi said, "I already have my greatest wish, which is to serve you. But if I could make another wish, I would wish to be taller."

The princess struck the hammer. She did not tell him that she too had made a wish, for right then, Isun Boshi began to grow taller and taller.

That night, when the princess told her father how brave Isun Boshi had been, the lord was so happy that his daughter had been saved that she found her wish granted, too. She and Isun Boshi could marry.

Paul Revere's Ride
BY HENRY WADSWORTH LONGFELLOW

Listen, my children, and you shall hear
Of the midnight ride of Paul Revere,
On the eighteenth of April, in Seventy-five;
Hardly a man is now alive
Who remembers that famous day and year.

He said to his friend, "If the British march
By land or sea from the town tonight,
Hang a lantern aloft in the belfry arch
Of the North Church tower as a signal light—
One, if by land, and two, if by sea;

And I on the opposite shore will be.
Ready to ride and spread the alarm
Through every Middlesex village and farm,
For the country folk to be up and to arm."

Then he said, "Good night!" and with muffled oar
Silently rowed to the Charlestown shore,
Just as the moon rose over the bay,
Where swinging wide at her moorings lay
The *Somerset*, British man-of-war;
A phantom ship, with each mast and spar
Across the moon like a prison bar,
And a huge black hulk, that was magnified
By its own reflection in the tide.

Meanwhile, his friend, through alley and street,
Wanders and watches, with eager ears,
Till in the silence around him he hears
The muster of men at the barrack door,
And the measured tread of the grenadiers,
Marching down to their boats on the shore.

Then he climbed the tower of the Old North Church,
By the wooden stairs with steady tread,
To the belfry-chamber overhead,
And startled the pigeons from their perch
On the somber rafters, that round him made
Masses and moving shapes of shade
By the trembling ladder steep and tall
To the highest window in the wall,
Where he paused to listen and look down
A moment on the roofs of the town,
And the moonlight flowing over all.

Beneath in the churchyard, lay the dead,
In their night-encampment on the hill,
Wrapped in silence so deep and still

That he could hear, like a sentinel's tread,
The watchful night-wind, as it went
Creeping along from tent to tent,
And seeming to whisper, "All is well!"
A moment only he feels the spell
Of the place and the hour and the secret dread
Of the lonely belfry and the dead;
For suddenly all his thoughts are bent
On a shadowy something far away,
Where the river widens to meet the bay
A line of black that bends and floats
On the rising tide like a bridge of boats.

Meanwhile, impatient to mount and ride,
Booted and spurred, with a heavy stride
On the opposite shore walked Paul Revere.
Now he patted his horse's side,
Now he gazed at the landscape far and near,

Then, impetuous, stamped the earth,
And turned and tightened his saddle girth;
But mostly he watched with eager search
The belfry tower of the Old North Church,
As it rose above the graves on the hill,
Lonely and spectral and somber and still.
And lo! as he looks, on the belfry's height
A glimmer, and then a gleam of light!
He springs to the saddle, the bridle he turns,
But lingers and gazes, till full on his sight
A second lamp in the belfry burns!

A hurry of hoofs in a village street,
A shape in the moonlight, a bulk in the dark,
And beneath, from the pebbles, in passing, a spark
Struck out by a steed flying fearless and fleet:
That was all! And yet, through the gloom and the light,
The fate of a nation was riding that night;
And the spark struck out by that steed, in his flight,
Kindled the land into flame with its heat.
He has left the village and mounted the steep,
And beneath him, tranquil and broad and deep,
Is the Mystic, meeting the ocean tides;
And under the alders that skirt its edge,
Now soft on the sand, now loud on the ledge,
Is heard the tramp of his steed as he rides.

It was twelve by the village clock,
When he crossed the bridge into Medford town.
He heard the crowing of the cock,
And the barking of the farmer's dog,
And felt the damp of the river fog,
That rises after the sun goes down.
It was one by the village clock,
When he galloped into Lexington.
He saw the gilded weathercock
Swim in the moonlight as he passed,

And the meeting-house windows, blank and bare,
Gaze at him with a spectral glare,
As if they already stood aghast
At the bloody work they would look upon.

It was two by the village clock,
When he came to the bridge in Concord town.
He heard the bleating of the flock,
And the twitter of birds among the trees,
And felt the breath of the morning breeze
Blowing over the meadows brown.
And one was safe and asleep in his bed
Who at the bridge would be first to fall,
Who that day would be lying dead,
Pierced by a British musket-ball.

You know the rest. In the books you have read
How the British Regulars fired and fled—
How the farmers gave them ball for ball,
From behind each fence and farmyard wall,
Chasing the red-coats down the lane,
Then crossing the fields to emerge again
Under the trees at the turn of the road,
And only pausing to fire and load.
So through the night rode Paul Revere;
And so through the night went his cry of alarm
To every Middlesex village and farm—
A cry of defiance and not of fear,

A voice in the darkness, a knock at the door,
And a word that shall echo forever more!
For, borne on the night-wind of the Past,
Through all our history, to the last,
In the hour of darkness and peril and need,
The people will awaken and listen to hear
The hurrying hoof-beats of that steed,
And the midnight message of Paul Revere.

Peter Pan

One night Mrs. Darling found a boy's shadow caught in the window latch. She folded it and hid it in a drawer. Then she and Mr. Darling went out for the evening.

Mr. Darling had gotten angry with Nana the dog and sent her to her kennel, so the dog wasn't there to frighten the boy away. He flew right in through the window as soon as the parents were gone. He was dressed in a ragged tunic of green and brown, and his hair was wild. In his belt he carried a set of pipes for playing music, and at his side flew a little fairy named Tinkerbell.

Tinkerbell showed the boy where to find his shadow. Then he tried to stick it on with soap. But seeing it was no use, the boy began to cry, waking Wendy, the oldest of Mr. and Mrs. Darling's three children. She quickly sewed the shadow back on.

He told her that he was Peter Pan, and that he lived in a place called Never Land where he was leader of the Lost Boys. In Never Land they played all day and had adventures with the Indians and the pirates. The best thing about Never Land, he said, was that there you could remain a child forever. Peter convinced Wendy to come to Never Land to be mother to the Lost Boys. Her brothers John and Michael were to come along. After sprinkling them with fairy dust, he led them flying through the night.

The Lost Boys were overjoyed to have a mother at last. In their secret underground house, Wendy cooked pretend meals, mended holes in the boys' clothes, told them bedtime stories, and made sure that they took their medicine every night. Meanwhile, John and Michael stalked Indians and fought pirates with Peter and the others every day.

The pirates' leader was Captain Hook, so named because in the place where one of his hands should have been there was a deadly hook. Captain Hook had lost his hand during a fight with Peter Pan. Peter had cut off the hand and thrown it to a crocodile lurking near the ship. Since that day, the crocodile had followed Hook, hoping to get another taste of him; and the croc might have succeeded, were it not for the fact that he had somehow swallowed a clock that ticked loudly. Hook could hear the croc sneaking along, so he always escaped his terrible jaws.

One night Wendy told the Lost Boys all about the home she and her brothers had left behind. She wanted to go home, and all the boys wanted to go with her. All except Peter Pan, that is. They decided to go without him. They didn't know that the pirates had discovered Peter's hiding place and were waiting for a chance to take revenge. As Wendy and the boys stepped outside, the pirates grabbed them one by one and carried them off.

Meanwhile down below, Peter had gone to sleep. Down a hollow tree crept Captain Hook to pour poison into the glass of medicine which Wendy had left for Peter to take. When Peter awoke, he reached for the glass and lifted it to his mouth. But before he could drink it, Tinkerbell saved Peter's life by drinking the deadly stuff herself. Peter saw her light beginning to fade. "Please," he cried to all children everywhere. "You must clap your hands and say, 'I do believe in fairies!'" Tink's light began to grow brighter again. The children were doing as Peter had said! Tinkerbell was saved.

Tink told Peter what had happened, and he rushed to rescue Wendy and the boys from Hook's ship. Peter hid in the ship's hold and made strange noises. Frightened by the noises, the pirates sent their captives John, Michael, and the Lost Boys inside to face whatever it might be. Then all grew quiet.

Suddenly the door burst open and out came Peter with his boys. They attacked, and soon all the pirates but Hook were captured or had run away. "Leave Hook to me!" shouted Peter Pan. The two faced each other with swords drawn. Back and forth they fought, hatred gleaming in their eyes. At last Peter gained the upper hand, and with one sharp blow, he sent Hook overboard, right into the jaws of the waiting crocodile.

Though he refused to leave Never Land for good, Peter agreed to fly Wendy home with the boys. Imagine Mrs. Darling's face when her long lost children came flying into the nursery, bringing so many new brothers with them! Wendy begged Peter to stay with them. He said no, but he promised to return every year to fetch Wendy to help him with his spring cleaning.

As the years passed, Wendy went back to Never Land from time to time. And when at last she had become much too grown-up to go flying off with the magical little boy, she sent her own little girl Jane in her place.

Robin Hood

Robin Hood and his band of merry outlaws lived in Sherwood Forest, where they robbed from the rich to give to the poor. The rich men of nearby Nottingham feared Robin Hood. Traveling through Sherwood Forest, they might find themselves suddenly surrounded by outlaws dressed in green, with bows drawn and arrows aimed. Since Robin and his men were the best marksmen in the land, the travelers dared not put up a fight. They handed over their money, which the outlaws divided among the poor.

One May morning, as the wild roses filled the warm air with their fragrance, Robin Hood walked through the green wood. He came to the narrow log bridge that crossed a rushing stream just at the moment that another fellow reached the bridge on the other side. Both wished to cross first. Even though the other man was seven feet tall, Robin was not afraid. They began to fight with staffs cut from a green oak tree. Soon Robin gave the other fellow such a crack on the head that blood appeared. But the stranger gave Robin a worse blow, knocking him into the stream.

Robin waded out, put his horn to his lips, and blew a loud blast. Suddenly his men were all around him. "What ails thee, master?" they said. "You seem to be wet to the skin! We will give this villain a good ducking, never fear."

Robin laughed and said, "No, let him go, for he is a brave fellow." Then to the stranger he said, "I am Robin Hood."

"My name is John," said the huge man.

"Well, 'little' John," said Robin merrily, "if you will wear green with us and join our band, I welcome you." John agreed, and so it was that he came to be known as Little John, one of the strongest and bravest of Robin Hood's men.

Among Robin's men was a fine singer named Allan a Dale. He was sad because his true love, fair Ellen, could not marry him. Her father insisted that she marry rich old Sir Stephen instead, a man whom

she did not love at all. Vowing to bring Allan and Ellen together, Robin Hood asked for help from a jolly priest named Friar Tuck. Together they went to the church, where Ellen was to marry Sir Stephen. The bishop began the wedding ceremony. "Stop the wedding," shouted Robin Hood, "for it is shameful to marry a maid against her will!" Fair Ellen's father, Sir Stephen, and the bishop were amazed to see the men in green suddenly all around. But Ellen smiled to see Allan among them. "Your daughter wishes to marry Allan a Dale," said Robin Hood. "Will you give them your blessing?"

The father frowned. Then spoke Sir Stephen: "Though I love Ellen with all my heart, I would not force her to marry me. Please give her your blessing to marry this young man."

Seeing his plan had failed, her father at last agreed. But the bishop refused to marry them. Friar Tuck stepped forward. "Here is a priest to help you," he said. He pronounced them husband and wife; then he rang the bells to tell the whole countryside that the true lovers were together at last.

Robin Hood, Little John, and the other outlaws had many adventures. Sometimes they rescued innocent men from the hangman's noose. Sometimes they traveled to the King's court in disguise to compete in archery contests,

where they shot their arrows the straightest and won all the prizes. By the time the King realized who the winners really were, they had all escaped safely to Sherwood Forest. Neither the King nor the sheriff could ever catch Robin Hood for long, for either Robin outsmarted them, or his men came to his rescue. Robin Hood became so famous that the old songs about him are still sung today.

From Tiger to Anansi

Anansi the spider was small and the animals liked to make fun of him. At night, when the animals sat in a circle under the trees, Brer Snake would say, "Who's the strongest of us all?"

"Tiger," Parrot called. "When Tiger shouts the trees tremble."

"And who's the weakest of us all?" Snake would ask.

"Anansi," shouted Frog. "When Anansi shouts no one listens." And all of the animals laughed.

One night, Tiger and Anansi came face to face. The grass swayed and the branches trembled as the animals drew nearer to watch.

Anansi bowed so low that his forehead touched the ground. "Tiger," Anansi said, "I have a favor to ask."

Tiger chuckled. "What is it?"

"Tiger, we know that you are strongest of all. That is why we give your name to things. We have tiger lilies, tiger moths, tiger beetles, tigereyes, and tiger stories. But I am so weak, nothing has my name. Tiger, let there be something named for me."

Tiger's tail switched from side to side. "What could that be?"

Anansi didn't dare to look up. "The stories," he said. "The stories that we tell at night about Brer Snake and Brer Parrot and all of us."

Tiger liked these stories, and he did not plan to give them away. "Very well, Anansi. But you must do something for me. We will call the stories by your name if you can bring Snake to me. And you must bring him alive."

"Very well," Anansi said. And at that, the animals began to laugh so hard that Parrot almost fell from his tree. Tiger laughed loudest of all, for no one was smarter than Snake and no one more foolish than Anansi.

Anansi made a plan. The next morning he made a trap out of vine, and in the center of the trap, he placed Snake's favorite berries. Then he waited. Along came Snake. When he saw the berries, he lay across the vine and began to eat them. Anansi pulled on the vine, and pulled again, but Snake was too heavy and the vine wouldn't move. Snake slipped away.

The next morning, Anansi climbed high into the trees to pick the freshest bananas. He made a deep hole, made the sides slippery with grease, and put the bananas at the bottom. When Snake saw the bananas, he slipped

right by the hole, looped his tail around a tree branch, reached down, and plucked those bananas up without ever touching the slippery sides.

Anansi was discouraged. Snake looked up from his bananas and caught Anansi watching him. "Anansi," he said. "I am so mad at you I might just eat you on the spot. Why are you trying to catch me?"

"You are too clever, Snake," Anansi answered. "Because I can't catch you, I can never prove to the other animals that you are the longest animal of all."

Snake hissed, "Of course I am. Look, I am as tall as that bamboo tree." And he stretched his body long.

"I don't know," said Anansi. "That bamboo tree looks longer to me."

"Measure me," Snake said.

So, Anansi cut down the bamboo tree, lay it beside Snake, and said, "Snake, when I go up to see where your head is, you go up. When I go to see where your tail is, you go down. In that way, you will always seem longer to me than the bamboo tree. How can I measure you fairly?"

"Tie my tail," Snake said. "I know that I am longer."

Anansi tied his tail, and went to stand by Snake's head. "Now stretch, Snake," he said. "Just two inches farther."

All of the animals began to cheer Snake on. Snake stretched longer and longer. He stretched so hard that he had to squeeze his eyes shut. Snap! Anansi tied his head to the branch.

The animals fell quiet, and Tiger walked out from the trees. Yes, there was Snake, all tied up. None of the animals could laugh at Anansi again. And from now on, the stories of the jungle animals would be known as the stories of Anansi.

MYTHS FROM ANCIENT GREECE AND ROME

Now we are going to tell you about the myths of the Greeks and Romans who lived about two thousand years ago. They lived near the Mediterranean Sea, which divides Europe from Africa. See if you can find the Mediterranean Sea on a map, and then you can find Greece and Rome.

The ancient Greeks and Romans are still important because they gave us many of our ideas. The way our government works comes from Greece. It's called democracy. The "demo" part of demo-cracy is taken from the Greek word for people, and the "cracy" part of demo-cracy is taken from the Greek word for power or rule. Put the two words together, and you get "the rule of the people"—exactly what democracy is.

Myths That Explain the World

Many Greek and Roman myths are stories that explain why things happen in the world. They explain why it gets cold in the winter and hot in the summer. They explain why there are floods and volcanoes. They explain rainbows and stars. These stories are called explanation myths.

Many Greeks and Romans believed these stories. They didn't call them myths. Stories are called myths only when people don't believe them anymore. Today, science gives us different explanations of how things happen. But people still talk about the old myths, which are some of the most interesting stories we know.

The Gods and Goddesses

The ancient Greeks and Romans used to say that the gods and goddesses lived on a tall mountain, called Mount Olympus, high above the clouds. The gods

ate and feasted every day in a great hall on Mount Olympus, ruled over by the king and queen of the gods.

These gods and goddesses looked and acted much like people, except that they had magical powers, and lived forever. They also watched what was going on down below with people on earth, and would help those they liked, or punish those they didn't. If someone was good at playing games, or someone else made a fortune quickly, the Greeks believed it was because the different gods were helping. This is the way the Greeks and Romans explained things around them.

Introducing Some Gods and Goddesses

These are some of the gods and goddesses who appear in the old stories and myths. We will introduce the main ones to you right away, so you will recognize them when they appear in the stories. You will see that the Greeks and Romans often had different names for the same gods.

Zeus

Zeus was the king of the gods. The Romans called him Jupiter. He controlled the heavens, and decided disputes among the gods. The ancient Greeks and Romans thought that when there was lightning and thunder it was the god Zeus (Jupiter) throwing a mighty thunderbolt!

Hera

Hera was not only the wife of Zeus, she was also his sister. In fact, most of the gods were brothers and sisters of Zeus, or else his sons and daughters. Hera was the queen of the gods, and the goddess of marriage. The Romans called her Juno.

Apollo

The sun was controlled by the god Apollo, a son of Zeus. The reason that the sun rose every day and traveled across the sky was because Apollo carried it across the sky in a golden chariot. The chariot was pulled by mighty horses, which rested at night so they could make their long journey again the next day.

Poseidon

Why was the ocean sometimes calm, and other times rough, with great high waves that could cause a shipwreck? Because of Poseidon, the powerful god of the sea. He lived underwater with the fish and mermaids and other

sea creatures. If he liked you, he would give you smooth sailing, but if he didn't, or if he was in a bad mood, look out! He could toss you about, as though your ship were a toy. Poseidon is pictured with a long beard and holding a trident, a kind of large pitchfork with three prongs. The Romans called him Neptune.

Aphrodite and Eros

Why do people fall in love? The ancients thought it was because of the goddess of love and beauty. The Greeks called this goddess Aphrodite and the Romans called her Venus. She was the most beautiful goddess of all. She had a son the Greeks called Eros. You probably know him by his Roman name, Cupid. What does Cupid look like?

When Aphrodite wanted someone to fall in love, she ordered Eros to shoot that person with one of his magic arrows. For if he hit you with an arrow, you would fall in love forever with the first person you saw.

Ares

Aphrodite was an expert in love, but Ares was the god of war. The Romans, who were great warriors, thought this god was very important. They called him Mars and thought of him as an excellent soldier who would fight for those people on earth whom he favored.

Hermes

The gods needed a messenger to carry their commands to humans, and they appointed the god Hermes, another son of Zeus, for that job. The Romans called him Mercury. Hermes is pictured with wings on his hat and sometimes on his sandals to show how fast he traveled.

Hephaestos

Hephaestos was the god of fire. He could cause volcanoes, making the earth spit up hot flames and glowing lava. The Romans called him Vulcan and named volcanoes after him. But he used fire in other ways. He could heat metal in his fire, and forge armor, and swords, and spears. He could also make beautiful golden cups to drink from, and shining jewelry. Hephaestos was lame, and spent his time working at his fiery forge.

Athena

The Greeks had a special goddess called Athena, who guarded one of their cities, Athens. She was the goddess of wisdom, and was wise from the day she was born. One day Zeus had a terrible headache. He complained to Hephaestos, who took his hammer and struck Zeus on the head. And from Zeus's head jumped Athena, already grown-up, and dressed in armor! The Romans called this goddess Minerva.

Hades

The Greeks and Romans believed that when people died they went to a shadowy place underground ruled by one of the gods. The Greeks called this ruler of the dead Hades and even named the underworld Hades after him. The Romans called this god Pluto.

Earth Goddesses

The earth we live on seemed so wonderful to the Greeks that they thought of it as a goddess named Ge. The study of the earth is called geology, after her. Because food comes from the earth, the Greeks saw Ge as a mother who fed them all, her children. Many other peoples and tribes have seen the earth that way. Even today we speak of Mother Earth.

Another earth goddess was Demeter, who protected agriculture and all the fruits of the earth. For the Romans her name was Ceres. Your breakfast cereal is named after Ceres. The ancient Greeks and Romans told a story about her, which we are going to tell you, that explained why it gets cold in winter and plants die, and why they come back to life in the springtime.

CERES

Demeter and Persephone

Demeter was the goddess of the harvest, the gathering of ripe fruits and vegetables. People loved Demeter because she was kind and generous and gave them plenty of food. It was because of her that corn and other grains grew in the fields, and the earth was green.

Demeter had a daughter, called Persephone, whom she loved very much. One day, Hades, the god of the underworld, was riding over the earth, and he saw Persephone. She was so beautiful and friendly—as she was to everyone she met—that he fell in love with her right there. He asked her to marry him and come to his kingdom in the underworld and be his queen. But she loved her mother and the beautiful earth she lived on, and she didn't want to go with him to the underworld.

Hades didn't care. He wanted her with him. So he swooped her into his chariot and carried her down into the underworld. Persephone was scared and very unhappy. The underworld was like a great cave that went on forever, all dark and shadowy. Oh, how Persephone longed to be with her mother, and run across the bright green fields.

Soon her mother, Demeter, noticed she was gone, and raised a cry of alarm. Demeter searched and searched for Persephone, but she couldn't find her anywhere. Demeter loved her daughter more than anything in the world, and she couldn't bear to be without her. She asked the other gods if they had seen her daughter. Apollo, the god of the sun, told her he had seen Hades carry Persephone off to the underworld in his chariot.

Demeter became very sad. She no longer went to the great feasts with the other gods and goddesses on Mount Olympus. She no longer laughed or drank sweet ambrosia from golden cups beside her friends and sisters. She no longer cared for her beautiful earth or the bright yellow grains that were her treasure. She went off by herself to weep for her daughter. And the earth became cold and bare. The golden corn died. Soon the people everywhere became hungry, because they had no grain or fruit to eat.

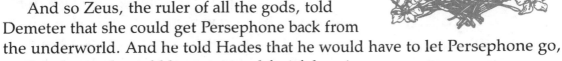

And so Zeus, the ruler of all the gods, told Demeter that she could get Persephone back from the underworld. And he told Hades that he would have to let Persephone go, so that the earth could be warm and fruitful again.

But Hades loved Persephone and didn't want to let her go. So he gave Persephone a magical pomegranate, a fruit red on the outside like an apple but full of small fruit-covered seeds on the inside. Because Persephone ate part of the pomegranate, she had to stay in the underworld with Hades for part of every year. And during these months, the earth gets cold, winter comes, and the plants retreat into the earth, just like Persephone. But when Persephone returns from Hades, spring comes and flowers bloom, and Demeter makes the earth bright with her happiness. This, the Greeks thought, is why the earth is cold during the winter, and warmer in the rest of the year.

Prometheus and Pandora

The ancients had a story that explained why there are bad things in the world. According to their myths, Prometheus, a powerful giant, loved mankind very much. And Prometheus saw that men needed help to stay warm and to fight the many fierce animals around them. So he went up to the workshop of Hephaestos, the god of fire. Prometheus stole some of Hephaestos's fire and gave it to mankind.

When Zeus, the ruler of the gods and heaven, saw this, he was very angry, because fire was supposed to belong only to the gods.

Zeus became envious of men, who now had fire. So he made the first woman, called Pandora. He made her very beautiful and gave her a golden box. He told her never to open the box. But when Pandora got to earth, she became very curious about what was in it. So she opened it, and out flew all the bad things in the world, things like pain, and disease, and mosquitoes, and earthquakes. One more thing came out of Pandora's box. That was Hope. Hope is the one thing that keeps people going, despite all the bad things in the world.

Zeus was still angry at Prometheus for stealing fire from the gods. So he bound Prometheus up and chained him to a tall cliff, where a great eagle clawed and pecked at him. Some say Prometheus was bound there forever. Others say he was eventually freed.

The Search Story

Have you ever wanted to see what was around the next corner, or just over the next hill? Have you ever wanted to go on a long journey and visit strange and different lands, and return to your home warm and safe? Have you ever dreamed of finding lost treasure, or being hailed as a hero by your friends and neighbors? These are dreams that people have had for many years.

You will find this kind of story throughout the world. It is called a quest myth. Quest means search. In a quest myth, a person leaves home in search of a treasure or something else that must be found. They have to travel through strange lands and brave many dangers before they can find what they are looking for. Often they have to fight foes and monsters to reach their goal. And once they have found what they are looking for, they must make the long journey home again, keeping the treasure safe. When they finally return, they are welcomed home and greeted as heroes and heroines. The ancients told a quest myth about a hero named Jason.

The Quest of the Golden Fleece

The most famous quest myth from ancient Greece is called the Quest of the Golden Fleece. It is about Jason and his men, who were called the Argonauts.

Jason was a handsome, brave young prince. His kingdom had been stolen from him by his uncle, an evil man named Pelias. Jason had grown up far away

from his kingdom, so one day he set out to regain the land that belonged to him.

Now Pelias, who had stolen the kingdom, had been told that Jason would come and try to take it back. And he had been told that Jason would be wearing only one sandal.

When Jason crossed the river into the kingdom, he lost a sandal. So when Pelias saw him, he recognized him at once. But everyone in the kingdom loved Jason, so Pelias did not dare to hurt him. Great crowds gathered around Jason in wonder as he walked through the city. Jason told Pelias that the kingdom belonged to him and that he wanted his kingdom back. And the people cheered for him and wanted Jason as their king.

But Pelias was as clever as he was wicked. He told Jason about a Golden Fleece, a wonderful magical fleece that had been the hide of a golden ram. Pelias said that the Golden Fleece had originally belonged to Jason's father, who was dead, and that Jason's father had asked Jason to bring the Golden Fleece home to his kingdom. Once Jason brought back the Fleece, he could be king.

The Golden Fleece was in a far distant land and guarded by a terrible serpent. This seemed like a wonderful challenge to Jason. It would be a long voyage, and there would be many dangers, but Jason was sure he could get the Fleece. Of course Pelias was hoping that Jason would be killed along the way.

Sailing with the Argonauts

Jason called together many of the greatest heroes in Greece to help him on his quest. The most famous of all was Hercules, the strongest man in the world. Another famous hero was named Orpheus, the greatest musician in the world, who played beautiful music on his harp. There were famous warriors, too, including the twins Castor and Pollux. The heroes built a ship called the *Argo*, and called themselves the Argonauts. They were off to seek adventure and the Golden Fleece!

Unfortunately, almost as soon as they got underway, the Argonauts lost Hercules. Here's how it happened. Hercules was so strong that he broke his oar while rowing the ship. So the Argonauts stopped off at an island to get wood for a new oar. As Hercules was chopping down a tree, his friend Hylas went off to get water. Hylas dipped his pitcher in a nearby stream, and a nymph, a water goddess who lived in the stream, fell in love with him. She reached up from the water and pulled Hylas into the stream to live with her forever. Hercules went to look for him and got lost, and the ship had to leave without him.

Then the Argonauts had to face the Harpies. The Harpies were horrible winged creatures that smelled terrible and stole the food from your mouth. The brave Argonauts defeated the Harpies, and saved a blind old prophet named Phineus from them. Phineus was so grateful that he told them where to find the Golden Fleece. He also told them about further dangers that awaited them, and how to overcome them.

He said that they would come to two great rocks in the ocean that opened and closed like jaws, smashing whoever tried to go between them. The way to get between them, he said, was to send a dove flying through first. If the dove got through, then they would too.

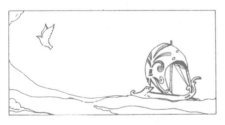

When the Argonauts did send the dove, it flew through. Only its tail feathers got caught in the rocks. When the Argonauts sailed through, they, too, made it. Only the very back of their boat was damaged by the rocks. From then on the rocks were permanently shut, no longer a danger to sailors.

They also sailed past Prometheus, who was chained to a tall cliff. An enormous eagle was clawing and pecking at him with its great beak, a punishment he suffered because he had brought fire to men. The Argonauts could not help him, so they sailed on their way.

They also passed by the island of the Amazons, women who were powerful warriors. Finally they reached the kingdom where the Golden Fleece was. It was ruled by King Aeetes.

Finding the Fleece

Even though the Fleece had belonged to one of Jason's relatives, Aeetes wanted to keep it for himself. So he told Jason that he could have the Fleece only if he managed to complete a difficult task. In fact, the task seemed impossible. But Jason wanted the Fleece, so he said he would try.

Jason's task was this: he had to tame two huge bulls that breathed fire. And then he had to make them pull a plow across a field. When they had plowed the field, he was to plant the teeth of a dragon! From the dragon's teeth would spring up an army of soldiers, which Jason had to fight alone!

If he could defeat the soldiers, King Aeetes said that Jason could have the Golden Fleece. The task seemed very hard, indeed. But fortunately Jason had help from the gods.

The gods and goddesses helped people that they liked. Hera, the queen of all the gods, loved Jason dearly. So she went to Aphrodite, the goddess of love, and asked her to help Jason. And Aphrodite did, in this way: she made the King's daughter fall in love with Jason. The daughter's name was Medea. Eros shot Medea with one of his love arrows, and as soon as she saw Jason, she loved him passionately.

Medea, even though she knew it would make her father angry, helped Jason with his task. She was a sorceress, so she could work wonderful magic. She gave Jason a special oil to protect him from the hot breath of the fire-breathing bulls. And she told him that if he threw a stone into the middle of the army of soldiers, they would turn and fight each other, not him. She told him she loved him, and Jason said that if he made it through alive, he would marry her.

All turned out as she said, and Jason completed his task. Medea took him to the Golden Fleece, which was guarded by a great, terrible serpent. But Medea lulled the serpent to sleep with her magic, and Jason seized the Golden Fleece. Then Jason and Medea and all the Argonauts escaped on their ship. They fled from the King Aeetes, who was angry that they had taken the Golden Fleece, and that his daughter had betrayed him.

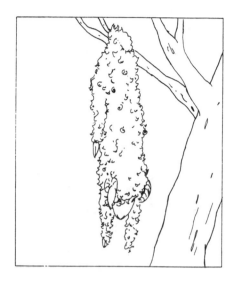

Aeetes sent his son after the Argonauts with a large army. Even though the Argonauts were great heroes, there were just fifty of them, against a large and powerful army. Medea helped to trick her brother, who was leading the army, so that Jason could slay him. This was how much she loved Jason. Their leader slain, the army went back home and the Argonauts escaped.

The Argonauts had many other adventures on their long journey home. But finally, with the help of Medea, Jason reached his homeland with the Golden Fleece. He was hailed as a hero, and was made king at last.

Introduction to Language and Literature

FOR PARENTS AND TEACHERS

In grade two, children should learn to identify and talk about nouns, verbs, prefixes, suffixes, antonyms and synonyms, and abbreviations. Experts say that our children already know more about the grammar of language than we can ever teach them. But *written* language does have special characteristics that need to be talked about with children. They need to learn the special conventions of written language.

To make the information really interesting, the child needs you. Such activities as asking questions, seeking new examples together, praising right answers, and playing guessing games will liven up the proceedings.

Young children love language. Identifying nouns and verbs should be child's play, and can be made more playful by making nouns out of verbs and verbs out of nouns. "Did you *lunch* with your friend?" "Did your friend's *eating* bother you?" You can make up prefixes and suffixes. "Did you *overlunch* and eat too much?" "How many *lunchers* were at your table?" And so on with antonyms, synonyms, and abbreviations.

The little section on literary terms addressed to children has the same function as the section on language: learning how to talk about language and literature in order to make progress in learning those subjects. Parents and teachers should be aware that the literature discussions can be usefully coordinated with the discussion of drama and playacting in the Fine Arts section.

Learning About Language

One Kind of Word: Nouns

Close your eyes and touch the things around you. The book. The chair. The bed. The floor. The names for these things are nouns.

When you're standing on the street corner, listen to the honking and the whir of the engines. These words for sounds, honking and whir, are nouns. On a summer day, smell the air and the grass that has been freshly cut. The names for smells are nouns.

The names for everything we hear or taste or touch or smell are nouns. The names for everything we see around us are nouns: the sky and the skyscrapers, the city and town, and the house or apartment where we live. Your own name is a noun. All names are nouns and all nouns are names for things.

Some nouns, like atoms and germs, are words for things that are so small that we can't see them. Some nouns, like fear and love, are words for things we can only feel. Nouns are very important. They are the first words a baby learns. After all, "Mommy" and "Daddy" are nouns.

Another Kind of Word: Verbs

Sing. Dance. Run. Jump. Laugh. Swing. Fly. Dream. These are verbs. Verbs are the words you use to describe everything you do from morning through night.

Verbs are also the words for making noises: the cars *honk,* the fire *snaps,* the thunder *cracks,* and the kettle *whistles.*

Verbs usually describe actions—what something or someone *does.* Verbs are what you do when you *run* as fast as you can and *slide* down the slide, or when you *hide* behind the house.

We use verbs when we *love* someone or *hug* them or *pretend* that they're not there. We use verbs to describe everything that happens. Try to say something without using a verb. Can you do it? Without verbs the world would be very quiet and very still.

Sentences

When you put a noun and a verb together, you make a sentence.

Take the noun "I," for instance, and then make a list of all the things you like to do, such as "leap," "drum," or "read." If you add the noun "I" to any of these verbs, you make a sentence.

Can you find the nouns and verbs in these sentences? Stars shine. Sound travels. Hearts beat. Spiders spin.

Prefixes

You can change some words fast by changing their beginnings.

Poof! and a *tricycle* becomes a *bicycle*. Tri- and bi- are called prefixes.

These prefixes tell you things. For instance they tell you about time. "Pre-" means "before," so when you add "pre-" to school to make preschool, it tells you that preschool comes before school. Some of the other prefixes that tell you about time are "mid-" as in midnight or midway or midday, and "after-" as in afternoon or afterward or aftertaste.

Prefixes can also tell you how many of something there are. If a tricycle has three wheels and a bicycle has two, how many wheels will you find on a unicycle? And how much sense does a parrot have if it's full of nonsense?

Prefixes can tell you where something is. The prefix "under-" tells you not to put your underwear outside your coat. The prefix "over-" tells you not to put your overcoat under your socks.

Suffixes

Suffixes are like prefixes except they go at the ends of words. Snap! and *"laugh"* turns into *"laughter."* You just have to add a few letters.

Suffixes are a lot like prefixes, but they can do even more things. Suffixes can change a verb like "act" into a noun like "actor." Add the suffix -ful to the noun "hope" and you have the word that describes the way you feel when you want to win a race: "hopeful."

Just add -er or -or to almost any verb and you have the person who did it, whether it's the sing*er,* or the sail*or* who got stranded, or the bat*ters* who set the batting records.

If you woke up this morning and forgot to tie your shoes, and left the front door open, your mother might say that you were mind-less. But if it didn't do any harm, she would say it was harm-less. And that's okay.

How many new words can you make by adding suffixes to words you know?

Antonyms

If you asked for hot chocolate, you wouldn't want it to be cold. Cold is the opposite of hot. To win is the opposite of to lose. Hot and cold and win and lose are antonyms. They are words that mean the exact opposite of each other. Lots of words mean just the opposite of other words. If you were to divide them up into teams, cold would be on one side and hot would be on the other. If you were to draw a picture of them, it might look like this:

cold .... hot

win .... lose

happy .... sad

Many words have antonyms. Some of them are easy: Up has down, and under has over. Good has evil, and far has near, and happy has sad. Many words have more than one antonym. The antonym for straight could be winding or curved or crooked. The antonym for small could be big or large or tremendous. Can you think of antonyms for tall, slow, and above? Can you think of some more antonyms?

The man is under the cow. The cow is over the man. What could have happened?

Synonyms

Synonyms are two words that mean nearly the same thing, such as pretty and beautiful. If you were to divide them up into teams, synonyms would all be on the same side.

We use synonyms when we've already used a word so many times, we don't want to hear it again. For instance, if a cat is ripping up the carpet and you've asked him to "leave" a hundred times, you could tell him to "exit" or "depart" or "move out." But he might really go if you said "git" or "scat."

---

*Y*ou can play a synonym game by yourself or with others. If you are in a group, divide into teams. One team thinks of a word, and then the players on the other team try to think of as many synonyms as they can. Be sure to count their answers. Next, the second team thinks of a word and the first team comes up with synonyms. After both teams take the same number of turns, you can see who came up with the most synonyms.

Abbreviations

Abbreviations save time by making words shorter. Every state, including yours, has its own two-letter shortcut. Michigan has MI and Minnesota has MN and Missouri has MO and Mississippi has MS. In fact, most addresses on postcards and letters have many abbreviations because when you address a letter, you include someone's title, such as Mr. or Mrs. or Ms., and the street, whether it's called a St. or Ct. or Ave. or Dr. or Ter. or Rd.

You can also use abbreviations when you're writing out measurements. When someone asks you, "How tall are you?" you can write ft. for feet and in. for inches. When you're measuring out sugar, use a tbsp. (for tablespoon) instead of a tsp. for teaspoon and you'll get a whole lot more. Once you start using abbreviations you'll see them everywhere. In the NFL and the NBA, the UN, and the U.S.A. You can even use them for your birthday. Just find the month on the calendar and learn the abbreviation for that month.

Learning About Literature

FOR CHILDREN

Folktales

When people first traveled to America from faraway lands like Africa and Europe, they brought with them tales that had been told by many, many people. Another word for people is "folk." So the stories were called folktales.

For a long time, the folktales they told weren't written down. They were

passed from parent to child, friend to friend. By listening to them, children had fun, but they also learned about good and evil, about how to behave, and about how things came to be.

These stories changed as they kept being retold by the different people who settled in our country. Dutch and French and English folk retold each other's stories. They heard and retold tales of the Native Americans. Early settlers invented new stories about adventures in the wilderness.

After a time, this country became a treasure chest of folktales. When you open a book of "American folktales," you'll find stories that started in other countries around the world, and also stories that started here. One kind of story that the early settlers told was the tall tale—a story so unbelievable that you weren't supposed to believe it.

Tall Tales

Have you ever stretched the truth just a little when you were telling a story? In a tall tale, you can stretch the truth a lot, and nobody will call it a lie. The more unbelievable your lie is the taller your tale will be, like the story of the fish you almost caught that was twenty feet long.

Some tall tales probably started with something surprising that really did happen. Maybe one time you really did almost catch a big fish a foot long. Then in your story it became twenty feet long. When people told about their adventures in the American wilderness, they made the happenings more amazing. Maybe one time a big wind called a tornado lifted a house from the ground and set it down again in one piece. Tall tales started about a man named Pecos Bill who could ride any tornado. Some men and women really could cut down trees fast. After a time, tall tales started about Paul Bunyan, who could cut down five hundred trees before breakfast.

Storytellers

The special person who remembered and told stories was a very important person in the times before people used writing. These storytellers kept alive the wisdom of the old times. In Africa, the storyteller was called the griot (gree-oh). In ancient England, the storyteller was called the scop (shope). Griots and other storytellers inspired their listeners with tales of bravery and tricks, often adding music or dancing. By keeping these stories alive through retelling, they gave people an idea of their history—just as if the storytellers had put old photographs on a table before them.

This storyteller of the Ibo people in Nigeria, Africa, wears a mask and costume and dances to tell his story.

Comedy

When you tell a joke to make people laugh, you are being a comedian, and the joke you act out is a comedy. You can find comedy in plays, movies, books, or in what people say who stand all alone on a stage and make the audience laugh.

Comedy can spring up in the middle of a story. For instance, in "The Emperor's New Clothes," it's funny that the Emperor's new clothes are really no clothes at all!

Some stories have parts that are comic and parts that are sad. Comic stories can talk about serious things, even sad things, like the clown who wears a sad face but makes us laugh anyway. Do you remember a story in this book that made you laugh?

Limericks

Listen to this limerick from Edward Lear's *Book of Nonsense*:

There was an old person of Ware
Who rode on the back of a bear:
When they asked does it trot
He said, "Certainly not!
He's a Moppsikon Floppsikon bear!"

The first line of a limerick often begins with "There was a" or "There once was a . . ." If you listen to the words at the end of each line, you'll see that the

rhymes fall in a pattern: (ware, bear), (trot, not), (bear). We call this pattern "A A B B A," because we use the letters of the alphabet to show the patterns of rhymes. A is the first rhyme, B is the second, and so on.

A   Ware
A   bear
B   trot
B   not
A   bear

Here are some lines all mixed up from a limerick by Theodore Roethke. Can you put them into the right order?

Who took only toads on his Back (A)
And go humping off, yickety-yak (A)
If you asked for a Ride (B)
He would act very Snide (B)
There was a most odious Yak (A)

Introduction to Sayings

Every culture has phrases and proverbs that make no sense when carried over literally into another culture. For many children, this section may not be needed; they will have picked up these sayings by hearing them at home and among their friends. But the category of sayings in the core knowledge sequence has been the one most singled out for gratitude by teachers who work with children from home cultures that are different from the standard culture of literate American English.

SAYINGS AND PHRASES

Better late than never.

People use this saying to mean that it's better that something happens late than not at all.

"Dario, I'm sorry we're so late getting to your birthday party. We had a flat tire."

"That's okay, Luke. Better late than never!" said Dario.

Better safe than sorry.

People use this saying to mean it's better not to take a chance than to do something that might be risky. They say this because you're less likely to be hurt or make a mistake when you're careful.

Bobbie dared Carlos to walk the railing of the old bridge.

"I won't," said Carlos.

"Chicken," Bobbie teased. "Go on, chicken."

"I'm not a chicken at all. I'm smarter than you are. Better safe than sorry," said Carlos.

A dog is man's best friend.

Some people think dogs make the best pets because they're loyal and loving. By calling a dog a friend, they show how highly they think of dogs.

What a terrible day it had been for Peter. He had

lost his math homework and forgotten his lunch money, and he had struck out twice in the softball game.

Then Peter heard his dog, Rollo, barking. Rollo jumped up and licked Peter with his big, wet tongue. "Rollo," Peter laughed, "you really are man's best friend."

Don't cry over spilled milk.

People use this saying to mean that once something is done or something is lost, you shouldn't feel sorry about it or worry about it.

"Hey, Greg, why so sad? You aren't still moping about losing the spelling bee, are you? Come on now, don't cry over spilled milk."

Don't judge a book by its cover.

People use this saying to mean that the way something looks may not tell you much about what it's really like. Or they use it to mean that the way a person looks may not tell you much about what that person is really like.

"Margaret isn't really prissy or stuck-up. She doesn't even like all those frilly dresses her mother buys her. She hates being the only one who dresses up for school every day. Just goes to show you, you can't judge a book by its cover."

Practice what you preach.

People use this saying to mean that you should act the way you tell others to act.

"Mom. Mom! *Help!* Ben took my train. He shouldn't grab my toys," Chris wailed. Then Chris yanked the train out of his little brother's hands.

"Boys, boys. Please stop!" said their mother. "Ben, you shouldn't take the toy Chris is playing with. And, Chris, if you grab things back from him, he will think it's okay to grab things from you. Please try to practice what you preach."

Two heads are better than one.

People use this saying to mean that when one person is having trouble with a task or problem a second person can often help out.

Pete was working on a puzzle of the fifty states. He had all the coast states along the edges of the puzzle, but the middle was still empty. "Rosie," he asked his sister, "what goes next to California?"

"Well," said Rosie, "Nevada and Utah? Or maybe Arizona."

"Nevada and Arizona both fit. Hey, thanks."

"Anytime," Rosie replied. "After all, two heads are better than one."

Where there's a will there's a way.

This saying means if you want to do something badly enough you'll find a way to do it.

"I can't believe our Girl Scout troop needs to sell six hundred boxes of cookies to top last year's record," said Hilary. "That's impossible."

"Oh no, it's not," said Tina. "Where there's a will there's a way!"

You can't teach an old dog new tricks.

People use this saying to mean that as you get older you get more set in your ways. Once you get used to doing something in a certain way, it becomes very hard to learn a different way to do it.

"Grandfather, why are you going this way to the market? Why don't you take the new road?" asked Mei Jing.

"Oh," laughed her grandfather, "I always forget that new road because I have gone this way to market all my life. I guess you can't teach an old dog new tricks."

Back to the drawing board.

People use this saying when something they're doing doesn't work out, and they feel as though they need to start over from the beginning.

"Ahmad, what are you doing?" asked his mother.

"I'm trying to write a poem for Kim's birthday. But it doesn't sound right. I think I need to go back to the drawing board."

Cold feet.

When we say someone has "cold feet" we mean he is afraid. People usually say this about a person who decides not to do something because he is afraid.

"I want to jump off the high diving board, but every time I try I get cold feet."

Easier said than done.

People use this saying to mean that it's sometimes easy to say what should be done, but it's harder to do it.

Rachel and Tom found a bicycle frame in a trash pile. "Let's take it home and fix it," said Rachel.

"Easier said than done," said Tom. "Where are we going to get two wheels and a chain to fit this bike? And how are we going to straighten the frame?"

Eaten out of house and home.

People use this phrase, often humorously, to mean that a huge amount of food gets eaten. The phrase implies that so much food gets eaten that someone may have to sell a home to pay for all the food.

"Are you excited that your sister is getting married?" Marie asked MaryJo.

"*I* am. My grandpa and grandma are coming to the wedding, and my aunts and uncles and cousins, too. But my dad seems a little worried. He says all Mom's relatives are going to eat us out of house and home."

Get a taste of your own medicine.

People use this expression to mean that someone who has been bothering or mistreating others gets treated in the same way.

"So, did Sakir play any tricks on you guys at school today, Rosa?" asked her sister.

"Nope," replied Rosa. "And I don't think he will for a while. He finally got a taste of his own medicine. During the school assembly we presented him with a medal for playing mean tricks. And *he* was really embarrassed."

Get up on the wrong side of the bed.

People use this phrase to mean a person is in a bad mood.

"Boy, was my mom a grouch this morning. I think she got up on the wrong side of the bed."

In hot water.

People use this phrase to mean in bad trouble.

"What was your favorite part of the movie?" Ryan asked Rita.

"I liked the part when they fell into the snake pit and the snakes were slithering all over them, and then the bad guys found them and sealed the pit," Rita said.

"Yeah," Ryan agreed, "they were really in hot water."

Keep your fingers crossed.

People use this expression in several ways. They say it to keep off danger. And they say it to show that they are wishing something so much that they are afraid the wish will not come true.

"What do you want for Christmas, Carmen?" asked José.

"Well, I'd like to have a bicycle, but I'm really keeping my fingers crossed that my grandmother will be out of the hospital by Christmas Day."

Sour grapes.

This phrase comes from a fable called "The Fox and the Grapes." The fox turns his disappointment against the grapes he can't reach, calling them "sour." So "sour grapes" means unkind or belittling remarks a person makes about something he or she can't have.

Jim asked his teacher, Mr. Rodriguez, "Why did Ron say our play isn't going to be any good?"

"Oh, that's just sour grapes," said Mr. Rodriguez. "Ron wanted to be the Nutcracker, and he's disappointed that he has to be one of the mice. But once he sees how much fun it is to dance around madly, he'll change his mind."

Turn over a new leaf.

To turn over a new leaf is to make a big change in the way you act.

"I've been late to school nine times already this year. But starting today I'm going to turn over a new leaf. No matter what happens, I'm going to be on time."

II.

GEOGRAPHY, WORLD CIVILIZATION, AND AMERICAN CIVILIZATION

Introduction to Geography

Americans of past decades, living in a large and relatively self-sufficient country, have had little incentive to gain geographical knowledge about the world that lies beyond North America. When the Korean and Vietnam wars began, few of us knew where Korea and Vietnam were to be found. As I write, American men and women are fighting a war in a part of the world called "the Middle East," which has been for many of us a geographically fuzzy concept. And our children tend to know even less about geography than we do. According to a study prepared by the National Geographic Society in 1988, our children are perhaps the only children in the world who know less geography than their parents do. This continuing and deepening American tradition of geographical vagueness, while understandable, has never been admirable, and is much harder to justify now that we participate in political and economic affairs that are increasingly global in character.

Unquestionably, the elementary school years are the best years to gain a permanent familiarity with the main features of world geography—the continents, the larger countries, the major rivers and mountains, and the major cities of the entire world. These spatial forms and relationships, when properly learned and connected with interesting stories, will remain unforgettable, as everyone who has good early schooling in geography will attest. Later on, as geographical understanding deepens, those early images become more fully correlated in our minds with an understanding of climate, agriculture, history, and culture. But the forms and spatial relationships that are learned early are the ones that remain most securely fixed in our minds. They become familiar and reliable patterns which we carry with us all our lives. They orient us when we encounter references to Sri Lanka or Malaysia or Ethiopia, or when someone asks how Israel can connect with Egypt when Israel is in Asia, and Egypt is in Africa. We would know the answer instantly if we carried a clear mental picture that Asia connects to Africa near the mouth of the Nile.

Such knowledge is gained by consistent map work that should include a lot of active drawing and coloring, and place-name identification. The association of shapes with names of places is at least as much fun as pinning the tail on the donkey. Committed teachers testify that the drawing of maps can be as absorbing as the drawing of pictures. Geography is and ought to be fun. But if the sense of the importance of geography is to be adequately conveyed to children, parents and teachers must be themselves convinced of the growing importance of geographical knowledge.

NOTE TO PARENTS AND TEACHERS: In the Geography, World Civilization, and American Civilization sections that follow, we several times mention materials from Dover Publications, Inc., which prints high-quality, low-cost coloring books, books, paper dolls, etc. Many of these are copyright free, and teachers can reproduce them for classes year after year. For a free catalogue write to Dover Publications, 31 East Second Street, Mineola, NY 11501.

World Geography

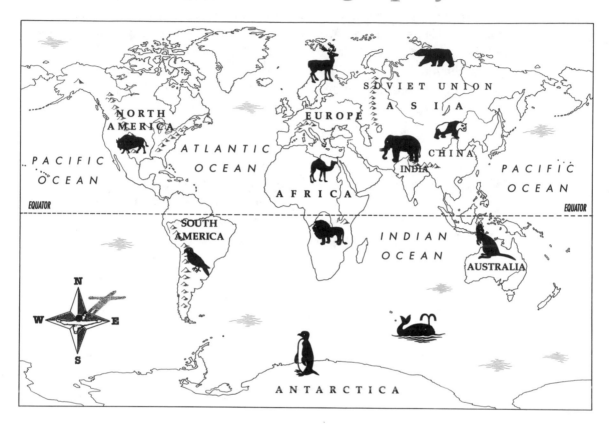

Mostly Water!

The world is like a huge ball. That's why we use a globe to study it. When we draw a picture of the world or one part of it, we call it a map.

Look at the map in your book or at a globe. You will see that most of our world is water, which is divided into oceans. Which is the largest ocean? Which is next in size?

The Third-Largest Ocean

Now look for the third-largest ocean. This ocean is north of Antarctica, with Africa on one side of it and Australia on the other. To the north of this ocean, what do you see? It is the continent of Asia, which is the largest area of land in our world.

Do you see a triangle that points like a finger out of Asia into this ocean? That is India, and it gives its name to this ocean, the Indian Ocean.

Seas: Mediterranean and Aegean

Do you see smaller bodies of water on the map? Some of these are called seas. The Mediterranean Sea separates the continents of Europe and Africa. A lot of what we will be learning in the next section happened around the Mediterranean Sea.

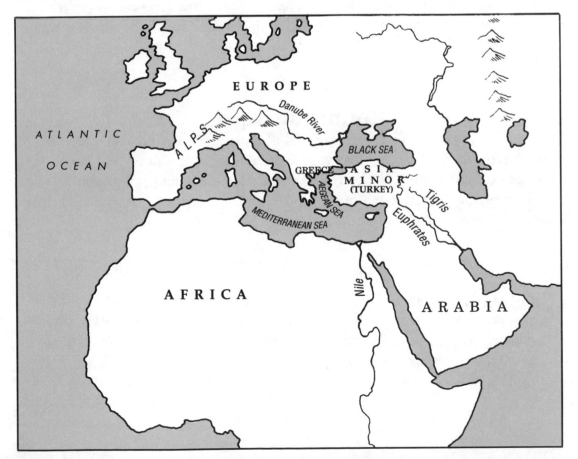

At the northeastern end (look right for east and look up for north) of the Mediterranean is a smaller sea called the Aegean Sea. On the western side of the Aegean Sea (look left for west) is the country of Greece. Across the Aegean, sticking out like a thumb, is a place that has been ruled by many different countries throughout history. This thumb is called Asia Minor, which means little Asia. Today Turkey is the country there.

> *A*sia Minor is a peninsula. A peninsula is a piece of land surrounded by water on three sides. When we study our country you will see that Florida is a peninsula. Have you ever heard of Florida? Can you find it on a map? Can you find any other peninsulas on the map?

Do you think there are a lot of oceans and seas to remember? You can stop now and trace the map and color the oceans. Then you can name out loud the places you've colored. You might even try to print a few of the shorter names on your map.

Continents Again

Can you name the seven largest pieces of land you learned last year? If you didn't have a book like this last year, you should learn now that these land pieces are called continents. In order of size they are Asia (the largest), Africa, North America (where our country is), South America, Antarctica, Europe (which is attached to Asia), and Australia.

> *C*an you think of an animal that lives on each continent? Can you print some of the names of the continents? You could print Asia. Also, you could go to your school or town library and find pictures of animals and mountains and rivers for each continent.

Remember that it is very cold at the "top" and "bottom" of our world. It is often very hot in many places along the equator. The equator is an imaginary line drawn around the middle of a globe.

This year we are going to learn about things that happened mainly on three continents: Asia, Europe, and North America. Can you find them on our map? And we will remember what we learned last year about the part of Africa that barely touches Asia. Can you find Egypt on your map?

NOTE TO PARENTS AND TEACHERS: We recommend a review of geography, world civilization, and American civilization in Book I of this series—*What Your First Grader Needs to Know.*

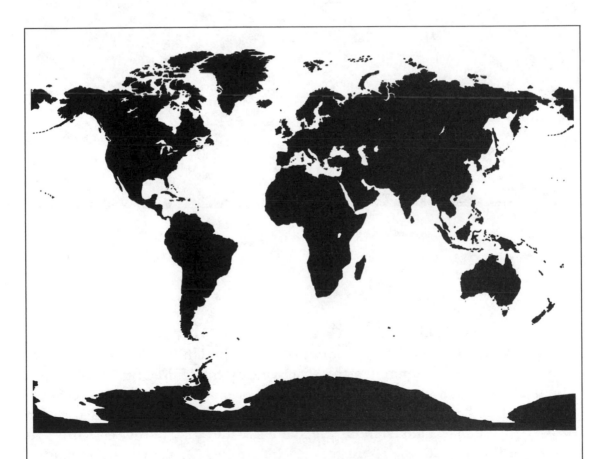

Point to the seven continents according to size: 1 = Asia, 2 = Africa, 3 = North America, 4 = South America, 5 = Antarctica, 6 = Europe, 7 = Australia.

Geography of the Americas

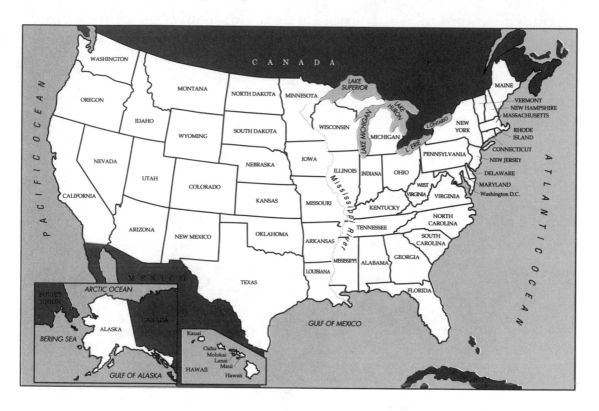

United States Geography

Let's take a long look at the map of our country, the United States, as it looks today. Do you see the different states that make up the United States? They are shown by lines that make little boxes and other shapes. These are the forty-eight states of the United States that are next to one another. Add to them Alaska and the Hawaiian Islands, which are separated from the rest, and you have all of the fifty states. There are also "territories," but they aren't shown on this map. They are islands.

In Alaska a herd of caribou migrates.

In Hawaii farmers often burn sugar cane fields before harvest to kill undergrowth.

Strange Shapes

When you look at all the states, you see that some have very unusual shapes. Can you guess why? For one thing, big rivers often separate one state from another, and rivers don't flow in straight lines. Let's think about rivers. They get bigger and bigger as they flow along. They start as streams, and grow as they join with other streams until they become a river. Then the river bends and twists around hills until it empties into a lake or a sea. As it makes these twists and turns, it forms the wavy line that separates some states from one another.

Lakes can give states odd

Look at the winding path of this river.

shapes, too. Do you see the big lakes in the north, on the border with Canada? They are called the Great Lakes, and you can see how they make the states there have outlines that aren't straight. The ocean doesn't follow straight lines either. Just look at the south of our country where a finger seems to be pointing down into the ocean. That's the state of Florida. Remember it's a peninsula, just like Turkey.

Some states are easy to remember because they are so big. See if you can find the big state of Texas. (Hint: look at the South again.) Another big state is California, the largest state out west on the Pacific Ocean. Can you find both California and the Pacific Ocean?

The First States

Today we have fifty states, but in the early years of our nation we had only thirteen. These thirteen original states are all near the East Coast of the country and the Atlantic Ocean. Why do you think the first people who came from England built their towns near the Atlantic? If you look at a globe, you can see that they had to cross the Atlantic. Where, in our country, would they have landed?

Let's look at the Atlantic Coast, and find the first thirteen states, one after the other. If we start from the bottom, the first state we see is Florida, but we have to skip it. It was Spanish and didn't become a state until later. Starting just above Florida, and going up we find the original English-speaking states: Georgia, South Carolina, North Carolina, Virginia (the first colony), Maryland, Delaware, New Jersey, New York (just a little piece of it is near the coast), Connecticut, Rhode Island, Massachusetts, and New Hampshire. But that's only twelve! What's missing? Is it the state at the very top? No, that's Maine, and at first Maine was part of Massachusetts. It's the large state just west of New Jersey. It's called Pennsylvania. Remember the Liberty Bell? That's where it is.

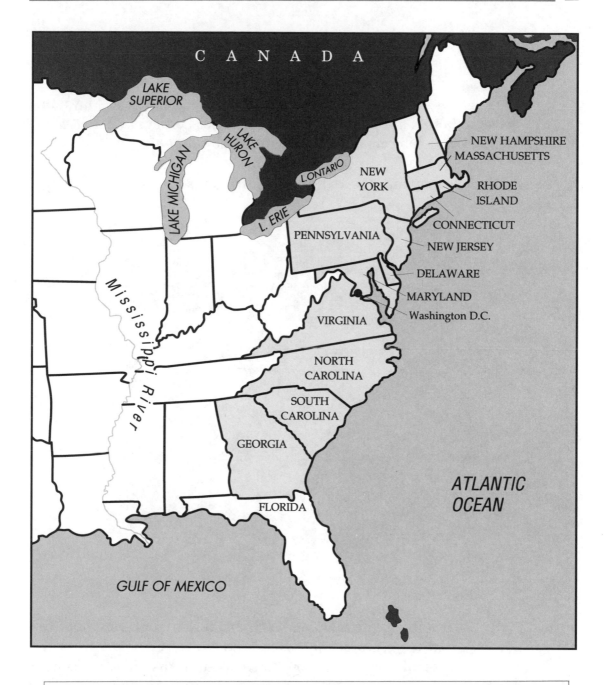

Trace the map of the United States and color the thirteen original states. See if you can remember their names. Also color the big states we talked about, and the state that's a peninsula, and your own state.

Geography of Mexico, Central America, and South America

NOTE TO PARENTS AND TEACHERS: We urge a review of the Inca, Maya, and Aztec sections of Book I in this series—*What Your First Grader Needs to Know*—or you can look these subjects up in a children's encyclopedia.

Let's look at the map that shows the places that are south of our country.

In these countries, the main language is Spanish. Do you remember that Spaniards conquered the cities of the Aztecs and Incas? Cortés with only a small army destroyed the main city of Native Americans in what is now Mexico. A Spanish explorer named Balboa went to Central America and set up a colony. He was the first European discoverer of the Pacific Ocean. Another explorer, Pizarro, defeated the Incas in South America. There were a lot of reasons so few Spaniards could conquer so many Native Americans. The

Cortés meets Montezuma, Emperor of the Aztecs.

Pizarro takes the King of the Incas prisoner.

Native Americans could not get together against the Europeans. They had no horses or guns. And, in later years, diseases brought from Europe killed millions of Native Americans. Because of Pizarro, Cortés and others, Spain owned what are now California and Texas and nearly all of the land south of our country. Spain owned most of these lands for about three hundred years. Can you see why most people in South America still speak Spanish?

There was one place that Spain did not own. In fact, it is the biggest country in South America. It's called Brazil. It was conquered by Europeans who spoke Portuguese, not Spanish. Both Spanish and Portuguese are called Latin languages because they are both based on the old language called Latin. Can you see why the countries south of the United States are called "Latin America"?

You can find the big country called Brazil if you look at the part of South America that bulges out into the Atlantic Ocean, the part that seems to point over to Africa. Notice that a big river flows through this big country on its journey to the Atlantic Ocean. It's the Amazon River, which carries more water than any other river in the world. When there is a lot of rain, the Amazon River can be thirty miles across! Around the Amazon is the world's largest rain forest. Scientists say that every person and animal on earth depends on this and other forests to "clean" the air we breathe. Did you know we are losing much of this important forest every year because people are cutting and burning it to build roads, mines, and farms?

Trace the map of South America. Now you can color the largest country. Do you remember its name? (Brazil.) You could make the second-largest country a different color. (Argentina.) What other continent does the southern tip of this country come close to? (Hint: It's terribly cold and has penguins.)

Do you have family or a friend from Mexico? Or from another country south of us? It would be fun to find out what celebrations their countries have on their birthdays.

Did you know that tacos are a Mexican food? You can make them with the help of a grown-up. Ask your parents to buy a box of tortillas. They are like pancakes made of corn. You can fill them with cooked ground beef or beans mixed with chili powder and tomato sauce, and topped with cheese. The box of tortillas will tell more about how to do it.

Independent Countries

Although people in these Latin American countries speak Spanish and Portuguese, the countries are no longer owned by Spain and Portugal. Their people decided to become independent, just as the people of the United States did. One of the leaders who helped them become independent had a country named after him. It's on the southwest border of Brazil. Can you find it? It is called Bolivia, after the great leader Simón Bolívar.

Simón Bolívar.

Simón Bolívar was one of the most famous leaders fighting for independence from Spain. He helped the peoples of five countries—Venezuela, Colombia, Ecuador, Peru, and Bolivia—gain independence from Spain.

In time, all the large countries of Latin America gained independence. Argentina, the second-largest country in South America, won its fight with Spain. Later on, Brazil became a republic. Mexico gained freedom about the same time as the South American countries. Mexico then claimed for itself all the land in North America that had been Spain's. Later, this land caused trouble between Mexico and our country.

Introduction to World Civilization

FOR PARENTS AND TEACHERS

In schools the world over, in Asia, Africa, the Americas, Europe, and Australia, young children are learning some of the same things about the history of human civilizations—about Egypt and other African civilizations, about Chinese history, the Babylonians, the Incas, Aztecs, and Maya, the Persians, Greeks, and Romans. Today, perhaps for the first time ever, children on all continents are learning not just the history of *their* ancestors, but also the broader history of all mankind.

This fortunate educational change may help reduce cultural conflict within and among nations. The study of world history is particularly appropriate in the United States where our population has come from every part of the world. To know world history is partly to know ourselves. The great American writer Herman Melville said about the United States:

> Settled by the people of all nations, all nations may claim her for their own. You cannot spill a drop of American blood without spilling the blood of the whole world . . . We are not a nation so much as a world.

The diversity of America is becoming the norm for other nations of the modern world. People from all over are to be found in almost every country, some to find better jobs, others to participate in international business. The modern international economy has turned the whole world into a single marketplace. The new global economy has created a new cosmopolitanism which makes it desirable that children in all countries, and especially in our own culturally diverse one, should share a basic knowledge of world history.

How reassuring it is to know that our children, by studying the larger history of mankind, will learn much the same history as children in other lands. The historical knowledge they will share will cause them to understand that people in every country have a common human heritage and a common stake in fostering a peaceful and civil world.

In this section, the topics include Babylon with its invention of writing, the rise of the Persians, the rise of the Greeks with their hero Alexander the Great, and the rise of similar civilizations in India and China with their own writing and heroes.

Again, you will find suggestions for activities that might help make the stories more vivid and memorable. These suggestions, which include recipes, role-playing, and titles of related books, can also serve as models for other activities you invent yourselves.

World Civilization

Cities Begin

Long, long ago, before cities arose, people moved around to find food. They looked for eatable plants and followed herds of animals that they could hunt. But once people learned to grow large amounts of food in one place, they could gather together to build cities. Last year we learned that the first cities were built next to rivers where water and rich soil enabled people to grow large amounts of food and stay in one place.

Cities were the beginning of civilization. In fact "civilization" comes from *civitas,* a Latin word for city. In cities, life became more interesting. People started having many different kinds of jobs besides the old ones of getting food, making war, and taking care of children.

Rock Painting of Deer Hunt.

In Cities: Different Jobs

What is one of the first things people need in a city? Places to live! This means there will be some people who just build houses and don't have time to grow food. Once the city is begun, there are many more new kinds of jobs. Can you think of some?

When large numbers of people live together, they need rules to get along, or laws. In different ways a person or a group will be chosen to make the laws and see that they are obeyed. These are the rulers.

Gradually people's jobs in cities become very specialized. Some people still farm, but others make clothes, cook, or clean. Some sell goods and food people no longer have time to make or grow for themselves. Others become artists, musicians, teachers, and scientists. All of these different special jobs began when cities and civilization started.

Ancient Peoples of the Mediterranean

Writing in Babylon

We already know from Book I that a great city called Babylon arose on the Euphrates River, in an area called Mesopotamia. Writing developed in this area, as it did in ancient Egypt.

Long ago people drew their letters or pictures on clay tablets like these.

Writing was one of the most important developments in human history. It allowed us to save and pass on knowledge. After the invention of writing, a young person seven years old could read about the many things humans had learned over hundreds of years. If you can read, you can know anything ever written down. After writing was invented, human knowledge could grow every year. The Babylonians used writing to study the stars and mathematics. You are learning writing and mathematics right now. So you can see how useful these ancient inventions are.

But Babylon, along with Egypt, was conquered by fierce invaders who came from the north. What were these invaders like? We are going to find out.

Important laws of Babylon are written on the tablet topped with this picture.

Tug-of-War: Caught Between Persians and Greeks

Have you ever seen two teams play a game of tug-of-war? (Your second-grade class could split into two teams to pull at the opposite ends of a rope. That's tug-of-war!)

Two energetic peoples, in Persia and Greece, arose and started fighting with each other for nearby lands. The people in places like Babylon and Egypt must have felt like the rope in a tug-of-war. This is the story of the struggle between the Persians and Greeks, and who won.

*P*arents and teachers may wish to order from Bellerophon Books in Santa Barbara, California, (805) 965-7034, two Bellerophon coloring books: Ancient Greece *and* Ancient Rome. *There is a Dover Publications coloring book that can be used as well: the* Aesop's Fable Coloring Book. *See the Introduction to Geography for Dover's address.*

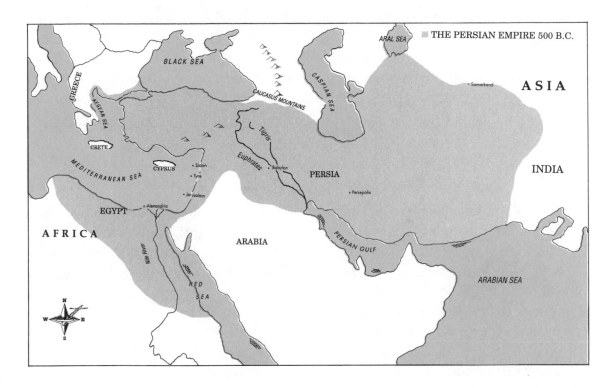

THE PERSIAN EMPIRE 500 B.C.

Persians: Where They Came From

Do you remember King Tut? Even before he was born, fighting people began to move southward from Asia, where the Soviet Union is now. (That's north of the Caspian Sea on your map.) Some went into India, some into Persia, some into Greece. Find Persia and Greece on your map.

We don't know why these people from the north began to move. Maybe they were hunting and following their herds. Or maybe they had heard

Here is a carving of a Persian man.

rumors of the wonderful cities and plentiful food of Babylon and Egypt. By 500 B.C. the Persians had conquered both Babylon and Egypt! The Persians quickly learned and copied the writing, buildings, and art of Babylonia. They "looked down" on trading but took a share of taxes from what traders earned in Babylon and Egypt.

Persian Boys Don't Lie

The Persians gave something back to the Babylonians and Egyptians. They gave all their different peoples one government, and coins, and a postal system. They believed in two forces, Good and Evil, rather than many gods. Instead of offering animals on the altars of many gods, a Persian honored the Good force by acting correctly.

As warriors, the Persians trained their boys to fight. The boys were supposed to learn three things: to ride a horse, to shoot with a bow, and to speak the truth. If a boy fell off his horse, he didn't pass to the next grade! Persian girls stayed at home, as girls did in much of the world until fairly recently. The girls did not go outdoors unless they went with an older person.

The Greeks: Jumping Over the Bull's Horns

The rivals of the Persians, the Greeks, also migrated south from where the Soviet Union now is, and they also found cities, just as the Persians had. The land they occupied became what is now Greece. The cities they discovered in that territory may have belonged to traders who had their headquarters on the island of Crete, where ruins of a great palace, where King Minos ruled, have been dis-

covered. (On the map on page 103, Crete is the large island north of Egypt.)

The Greeks were rough warriors, but they learned quickly how to build and sail ships. They mixed with the people already in Greece. Some people say they grew strong enough to attack Crete. The invading Greeks destroyed the palace on Crete and stole its treasures.

The Greeks have a myth which explains why they destroyed the great palace on Crete ruled by the legendary King Minos. From time to time, King Minos forced a Greek city called Athens to send boys and girls to Crete because, the story went, there was a bull called a Minotaur under the palace. These Greek boys and girls were trained to run and jump over the bull's horns and onto its back. Some were killed or terribly hurt. As you can see from the myth, the Greeks had a reason to be angry with King Minos.

Athens: Freedom's Birthplace

The ancient Greeks have left us certain things that no other ancient culture did. You already know that ancient peoples developed much that affects us today: agriculture, cities, writing, money, art, and architecture, to name just a few. The Greeks gave us other new ideas. And one of their most important ideas came from the Greek city of Athens.

Athens spreads out beyond an ancient building on the Acropolis.

Like other Greek cities, Athens owned farming land around it, and had its own army. So it was called a city-state. What made Athens special was her government. After hundreds of years of trying different ways of governing themselves, and arguing a lot, the Athenians agreed to give all citizens a share in governing. This was a new kind of government, in which the people chose their leaders themselves. And if their leaders began to seem dangerous, the people could vote to make them leave Athens. This was called "democracy," meaning government by the people.

Not everyone in the city of Athens could take part in the government. Over half were women and slaves who were not allowed to be citizens. They could not vote. But Athenian democracy was the beginning of the idea behind our country. And it is certainly different from having a king, or group of warriors, or priests giving laws. Where would you rather live? In a place where you helped make the rules (laws), or where you never had a say?

Sparta

Not every city-state in Greece was like Athens. Another leading Greek city was Sparta. The Spartans made captives of everyone who wasn't a Spartan. Then to keep so many captives from getting free, the Spartans had to live like soldiers all the time. But even Spartans had more freedom than Egyptians or Persians, because the soldiers elected many of their leaders.

The Spartans were great warriors. They were tough. Their soldiers' own mothers told them to come back from war either with their shield or on it. That meant they should either win or die. Have you heard the word Spartan before? If we call something Spartan, it's very plain and without frills. To live a Spartan life is to do things regularly like getting up early in the morning, taking a cold shower, or eating simple food without snacks. Another name for Sparta was Laconia. Since Spartans didn't talk much, the Greeks called un-talkative people "laconic." In English we still use "laconic" to mean "of few words." The Laconians were very laconic. Are you?

The Greatest Runner Ever

Besides Athens and Sparta, there were other city-states in what is now Greece. Greece had so many mountains, the city-states were cut off from one another. They didn't form one country, they fought a lot among themselves. This lack of unity gave Persia the idea she could conquer Greece easily. She had already conquered Greek settlements in many places.

So when the Persians attacked Greece they did not send all the ships and soldiers they had to fight—a big mistake! Still, there were many more Persians in these battles than there were Greeks. But the Athenians were able to defeat

Ancient marathon runners on a very old vase.

the Persians in a great victory near Athens at Marathon in 490 B.C. The anxious Athenians at home learned the result when a runner came all the way from Marathon to Athens, a distance of over twenty miles, to tell them they had won. The runner had not stopped once. After he delivered his message, he collapsed and died for his city. Have you ever heard of a marathon race? Now you know where it got its name.

A Huge Persian Army

After Marathon, the next Persian King decided to crush these annoying Greeks! Luckily, the Greeks had ten years to get ready. For once they worked together. The Spartans held off a huge force at a mountain pass called Thermopylae (Thur mop a lee). Every Spartan there died, but they fought so well the other Greeks gained courage. Thermopylae became a name that echoed through history as a symbol of bravery.

Even when the Persian army burned down Athens, the Greeks kept fighting. They waited for the battle to come at sea, where they had a better chance. Because they had used the ten years wisely, the Athenians had built enough ships to defeat the Persian navy. In fact, the Persians had too many ships, and they kept getting in their own way. That is what the Athenian leader had planned. The Greeks won. Soon Greece would be safe from Persia.

Olympic Games

Have you ever heard of the Olympic Games? They were begun in Greece and held every four years. They were a week long, and dedicated to the main Greek god, Zeus. The name Olympics comes from the mountain Olympus, where the Greeks supposed Zeus lived. Greeks came from all the city-states to run, jump, throw weapons, race chariots and horses, and to watch. It was like our Fourth of July because going to the games was an important part of feeling Greek.

In some ways the ancient Olympics were very much like today's Olympic games, but in some ways they were very different. At the ancient games there were contests in music and po-etry, which we do not have today. Also, the men wore no clothes, and women were not allowed to compete.

The prizes were also different. Do you know what the winner of an event in the Olympics gets as a prize today? She or he gets a gold medal. In the ancient games the winner got a crown made of olive leaves.

This is Joan Benoit, a modern marathon runner.

Poems, Plays, and History

The Greeks invented an alphabet different from ours that is still used in Greece today. The first two letters of the Greek alphabet are called "alpha" and "beta." Do you suppose that is where we get our word "alphabet?" The Greeks used their writing to record the great long poems of Homer about warriors and heroes, which we still read today. The Greeks also greatly advanced the writing of history. And they wrote plays. From Homer's poems, and from the words the actors spoke in the plays, the Greeks were taught what was good and evil. You can find out more about Greek plays in the Fine Arts section of this book.

| Alpha | A | a | ⋏ |
| Beta | B | β | B |

Athens: A Beautiful City

This is a picture of Pericles supervising building in Athens.

The Greeks were wonderful builders, too. During the leadership of a wise man named Pericles, the people of Athens built a new temple. It was to be the home of their most important goddess, Athena. They wanted it to be the most beautiful building ever made, and many people even today believe they succeeded. It was marble and decorated with beautiful statues. It was called the Parthenon, and you can read more about it in the Fine Arts section of this book.

Other Greek cities had fine temples, too. The Greeks were very proud of the new kinds of buildings they had designed. Many of the columns you see in buildings in our own country are copied from the decorated columns the Greeks designed.

Look at all the columns of the Parthenon.

F*ind photographs of Greek or Roman style buildings in magazines or library books with the help of a grown-up. Paris, France, and London, England, have many such buildings. Our own capital, Washington, D.C., is filled with them! Are there any classical buildings where you live?*

Pericles.

Asking Questions

The Greeks asked a lot of questions that had never been answered before. Some Greek thinkers wanted to understand how nature works. They were not satisfied to be told that the Nile floods because a god wants it to, or because a pharaoh orders it. One Greek thinker even figured out how large the world was and came very close to the right size! By asking questions the Greeks developed geometry and added new ideas to mathematics. Their questioning even led to the way of thinking scientists use today.

Not Smart Enough

Many Greeks were very curious, scientific, artistic, and athletic. They were more free to trade, own property, speak, and write than any people had ever been. The citizens of Athens could even decide legal cases and pick leaders from among themselves. Yes, there were slaves; yes, women did what they were told. But the Greeks were freer than any other ordinary persons in the ancient world.

For all their learning, the Greeks went back to fighting among themselves once the Persians were gone. The Golden Age of Pericles didn't last very long. Athens and Sparta fought a long war that Athens finally lost. Athens suffered greatly from this war and from a plague, which is a terrible sickness that kills many people.

Another Northern Threat

Sparta ruined Athens, and before long another city-state defeated Sparta. Now none of the Greek city-states was strong enough to stand up to the King of Macedonia in the north of Greece. For ten years an orator named Demosthenes warned the Greeks to unite. Finally they did, but it was too late. They were completely defeated, and the King of Macedonia ruled.

Alexander the Great

When the King of Macedonia died, his son, Alexander, was just out of his teens. One of the Greek cities tried to rebel against this new, young King. But

Alexander burned down the city and sold the citizens as slaves. After that the rest of Greece stayed quiet out of fear.

If the Greeks had known that Alexander would be called "the Great," they would probably have liked him more. But they didn't know he was going to take a small but tough army of Macedonians and attack the great armies of the King of Persia. They didn't know he would become the most famous general of the whole ancient world.

Why does this coin show Alexander with horns? Because many of his people thought he was a god and the ram's horns were sometimes traits of Zeus.

Alexander the Great.

Alexander as a Boy

Alexander was a very confident young man. He had been brought up by his mother to believe he would do wonderful things. He learned how to struggle, too. He grew up in a palace where there were a lot of rough warriors, and he learned to fight well.

Sometimes it seemed that the King might pick another son to follow him and not Alexander. So the young prince also learned how tricky people could be and how hard it was to stay a prince or a king.

The Greeks called almost anyone who wasn't a Greek a "barbarian," meaning a rough savage who could fight, but who couldn't read or write or appreciate anything "civilized." Does that make Alexander a "barbarian"? No! Alexander was very well educated by a very special Greek tutor. He had one of the greatest teachers the world has ever known, a man named Aristotle.

Alexander's Teacher: The Man Who Knew Everything

Do you know what an encyclopedia is? Your school library has a set of these books. You should go there and look at them as soon as you can. They can tell you what people have found out about *everything* in the world. Aristotle, Alexander's teacher, wrote the very first encyclopedia. He wrote down just about everything there was to know at that time. And he wanted Alexander to discover new facts wherever he went. He also tried to teach Alexander what was good and how kings should rule.

Aristotle had been the student of the great thinker Plato. And Plato was a student of the famous teacher Socrates, who wanted people to think for themselves. So Alexander had the best education available in the ancient world.

When Alexander took the army that his father had formed and left Macedonia, he

Aristotle teaching Alexander the Great.

wanted to do more than just fight. He wanted to discover new plants and animals for Aristotle. He may have even wanted to conquer Persia in order to rule it better. Perhaps he planned to be the kind of good king Aristotle had written about.

One thing is certain. Alexander wanted glory. That means he wanted everyone to know what wonderful things he'd done. For that to happen someone would have to go along with him and write everything down. You can pretend that you are the person he chose! Let's follow one of Alexander's war expeditions.

A Legend

Now you are setting off to the east on a horse Alexander has given you. After some days of riding you cross on ships to Asia Minor. You can look at a map to see how you would get from Macedonia to Asia Minor. Now you are in Persian territory and you stay near the end of the line of soldiers. Alexander doesn't want you to be hurt. You're supposed to write, not fight.

The first night in Asia Minor, as you cook your food over the campfire, you hear a strange story. One of the mythical kings of this land was supposed to have made a knot with so many twists and turns that nobody could untie it. It would be as though someone had tied your shoelaces so many times that you couldn't undo them. Only this knot was in a huge rope on an oxcart. There was an ancient belief about this knot, which was called "the Gordian Knot."

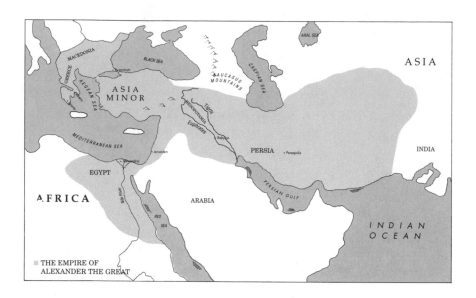

Anyone who could untie it was supposed to become the ruler of Asia. But no one had been able to untie it. The following day Alexander was going to try his luck.

The next morning you are allowed to ride in the front, alongside Alexander. He wants you to see him untie the Gordian Knot. But when you arrive at the oxcart, you see that Alexander is stunned. He isn't going to be able to untangle this mess unless he stays here a month, maybe a year. Maybe no one can ever untie it.

Alexander takes off his helmet and runs his strong fingers through his bright blond hair. He frowns and purses his lips. He scratches his big, sharp nose. Then his blue eyes flash. Pulling out his sword, he strides to the oxcart and cuts the huge knot in half with one stroke. The rope falls untied to the ground, and everyone cheers. You see that you will be writing about a man who thinks for himself, who does things the unusual way, and who is very determined.

Danger

But now comes the hard part. A large Persian army appears, and you go off to a hill so you can see what's going on. But when Alexander's much smaller army charges, all is hidden by a cloud of dust. Not until you see the Persians begin to run away do you know that Alexander has won.

Not all is happiness, though. Many are dead and wounded. You are sorry so many died. But the Greek cities are glad to be free of the Persians after more than a hundred years.

In the next two years you see the same thing happen again and again as Alexander marches to Egypt. Once there, he thinks the country so full of marvels that he starts a new city, which he plans to come back to later. This is the city of Alexandria near the Nile. It is still a famous port on the Mediterranean Sea.

Victory

Now you follow Alexander to attack the heart of the Persian Empire near the Tigris River. (Do you remember that river, where Babylonia was?) The Persian army is huge, but many of the soldiers don't know what to do. Many are not Persian at all. Alexander attacks, and many of his enemies run away, including the Persian King. The people of Persia accept Alexander as their King. He now is ruler of most of the ancient world.

Not Enough

But this is not enough for Alexander. He wants to go beyond the Persian Empire to India. At first his army is willing to go, but soon his men are stealing and arguing. You are unhappy to see them do more and more harm. While drunk with wine, they even burn down a beautiful city, an act which Alexander regrets. But still he goes on, fighting battles with strange peoples and getting wounded. Finally, the army refuses to go any farther. Alexander flies into one of his great rages, but this time the men are more afraid to go on than they are of him. Now they have to go all the way from India back to Babylon. Much of the journey is through desert, and they almost die. You are lucky enough to be sent back on one of Alexander's ships.

Persian soldiers used elephants to carry supplies and people.

A Very Big Wedding

While you wait for Alexander to return to Babylon, you hear he has tried to make up for some of the damage he has done. On the way back he has stopped at a Persian city to celebrate the largest wedding there probably ever was. Eighty of Alexander's generals marry Persian princesses. Ten thousand of his soldiers marry other Persian women! Alexander himself has already married a princess. The idea may be to show that Greece and Persia can get along.

A Sad End

You will not be able to see if Alexander's empire is better than the old Persian one because he does not live much longer. In fact, not long after he returns to Babylon, he dies of a fever. Right away his generals start fighting about who will rule.

Finally, Alexander's empire breaks up into three main pieces. Macedonia is the center of one part, Babylonia the second, Egypt the third. It has taken only ten years to make the empire, but it has taken even less time to break it.

You now decide it's time to return to the present, and say good-bye to the world of the Greeks and Persians.

Alexander the Great had a war horse, Bucephalus, so brave and strong that people believed it was given to him by the gods. If horses could talk, what a story Bucephalus would have told! You could make up a story about Bucephalus now that you know where he went and what he did.

Wonders in Africa: The Kingdom of Kush

Do you remember reading about ancient Egypt in Book I of this series? Do you remember pyramids, mummies, and the powerful pharaoh, King Tut? A long time ago in an area south of Egypt, there was a land called Nubia. To find Nubia, look at a map of Africa, find Egypt, then follow the Nile River south to the country called Sudan. This is part of the dry, hot region that was once Nubia.

In Nubia, there was a kingdom called Kush. Today, we are finding out about Kush with the help of scientists called archaeologists (ar-key-OL-oh-gists). Archaeologists learn about people who lived long ago by studying the things they left behind, like tools, weapons, and pottery. In Nubia, archaeologists have found a civilization more than three thousand years old, with beautiful temples and the remains of giant stone statues over two hundred feet tall! They have also found mounds as wide as a football field with royal tombs below, where kings were buried with their treasures.

The riches of Kush—gold, ivory, and more—attracted the attention of the Kushites' African neighbors, the Egyptians. Egyptian pharaohs sent their powerful armies south and demanded that the Kushites give valuable gifts to the pharaoh. As years passed, many Kushites adopted the Egyptian religion and some began to write using Egyptian hieroglyphics. Later, the kings of Kush, like the Egyptian pharaohs, built huge pyramids.

Eventually, the Kushites turned the tables on the Egyptians. Beginning in about 1,000 B.C., the rulers of Kush became more powerful, and in the eighth century B.C., a king named Piye (PEE-yay) led a great army northward and conquered Egypt.

A Nubian princess rides by a temple in Kush.

*C*hildren *will enjoy the photographs and drawings of artifacts from the kingdom of Kush in two magazines, the November 1990 issue of* National Geographic *and the June 1993 issue of* Smithsonian.

India

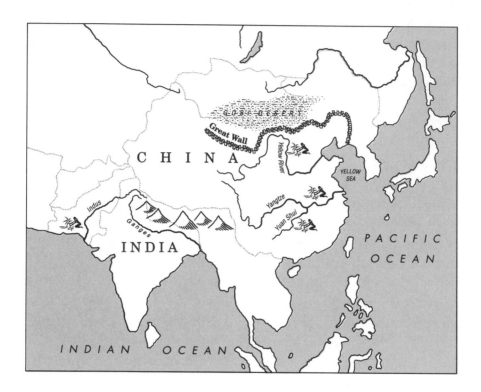

India's Rivers and Rulers

India's first cities were built near the Indus River. But for some reason that no one knows, Indian people left those cities a very long time before Alexander arrived in India. We don't know exactly what happened to these Indian people.

New people came into India from the north. We call these people Aryans. The Aryans lived in cities along a different river, called the Ganges River. They began to rule over the many peoples already in India.

When the Aryans first came to India, they talked a little bit like the Greeks and the Persians. Some of the Aryan gods were also like Greek and Persian gods. But the Aryans came to India over fifteen hundred years before Alexander did! By the time Alexander arrived, the Aryans had changed a great deal.

The Four Castes

When Alexander the Great arrived in India, the Indian people had already started dividing themselves into four groups called castes. This caste system was part of the people's religion, called the Hindu religion. The highest group was the priests; the second was the military leaders who owned the land. The third caste included people who owned stores and sold goods. They were called merchants. The fourth caste, the lowest, had to serve the others as laborers. Farmers, weavers, and barbers all belonged to the fourth caste.

People in India stayed in those groups and so did their children and grandchildren. When they married, they had to marry someone in the same caste. They also had to eat food cooked by people in the same caste! They were not ever supposed to change to another caste, even if they wanted to.

Now some Indians have different kinds of jobs and marry people from different castes. Modern laws have tried to change the caste system. But the caste system can still be seen in India today. There are many reasons why it is hard for the caste system to change. It is a part of the people's religion. Also, it divides up important jobs, so that all the things that people need to make a living will get done. It has been a part of people's lives for such a long time that it's difficult to change.

This Indian man is a potter; as a laborer he belongs to the fourth caste.

A Very Old Book Indeed

The importance of the Hindu religion to the Indian people is shown by a book of hymns and sayings written by Aryan men and women. This book is called the Rig Veda. The Rig Veda talks about celebrating weddings, funerals, and holy times. The Rig Veda is very old indeed. But the hymns and sayings were made up long before the book was written down. The Aryan people thought the hymns and sayings were so important that one of the priests' jobs was to memorize all the hymns so they would not be forgotten. This would be a hard job because there are over a thousand hymns in the Rig Veda!

If you were in India you could still hear people saying hymns from the Rig Veda at important times in their lives. In fact, the Rig Veda is the oldest book that people still consider sacred.

This is Shiva Nataraja, the Hindu god of dance.

The Story of King Asoka

One family of Aryan kings ruled almost all of India for a long time. Even though Alexander fought and won battles against the Aryan kings, he did not really take over India. Aryan kings soon began to rule again.

One of these kings is very famous. His name is Asoka. When Asoka was a young king, he fought lots of battles with his army. But after one war, he became sad because he realized that many people are hurt by battles. Even though Buddha had been dead a long time, Asoka heard about Buddha's teachings. You read about Buddha in the first book in this series. Do you remember that Buddha taught people not to hurt any living thing? Asoka listened to Buddha's teachings and stopped making war. He built hospitals all over India for people and animals. He told his workers to plant trees and dig wells for the people. He even set up houses along the roads for people who were tired from walking long distances.

Because Asoka believed Buddha's teachings, he decided that Indians should also learn more about Buddha. Asoka had Buddha's words carved on pillars and put them in places where many Indian people could read them. He also sent Buddhist priests in the direction of Greece and China to teach other people about Buddha's teachings. Because of Asoka, Buddha's ideas spread all over Asia and Buddhism is still an important religion today.

Even though Asoka believed strongly in Buddha's teachings, he said that kings should

Asoka had this statue of lions (called a capital) put up at the place where Buddha first explained his beliefs about peace. This capital has become a symbol for India in the same way the bald eagle has become a symbol for the United States.

let people worship however they wanted to. So Indian people felt they could worship their old gods and also listen to Buddha. This is one reason you can still see statues of Buddha next to statues of Hindu gods in Indian temples.

China
A Very Old Civilization

Last year we found out that people first built cities in China along the Yellow River (Hwang Ho) a long, long time ago. They had started farming in China before the pyramids in Egypt were built.

But then, many hundreds of years before Alexander went to India, Chinese people started building their cities between the Yellow River and the Yangtze River. Do you see these rivers on the map on page 120? People living there built large houses, created art, made fine silk clothes, and sent their children to schools. But many of the people were poor, because their rulers fought so often. Teachers like Confucius hoped that the fighting would stop. He explained that one single ruler would bring peace, make China stronger, and her people wealthier.

The Longest Wall in the World

The Chinese rulers thought Confucius had a good idea. But instead of working together, the kings all fought one another to try to be the one ruler. The kings also had to fight rough warriors from the north who were trying to invade China. One strong king decided to build a wall to keep out these rough warriors. Workmen started connecting walls that already existed. And for many years they added new walls to that, until they had a wall that was fifteen hundred miles long. The Great Wall is so long, it would reach from Maine to

The Great Wall of China.

Florida! Towers were built every few miles so watchers could look for invading horsemen. The watchers used smoke signals during the day and fires during the night to warn of trouble. The wall is still standing today.

Confucius's Hope Comes True

The wall did not keep out all the invaders from the north. But only a hundred years after Alexander built his empire, Confucius's hope came true. A ruler made the whole of China one country. Then a family of emperors called the Han dynasty kept China together for four hundred years! The Han emperors still warred with the invaders from the north, which meant many Chinese were still poor. But the emperors also learned to make agreements with the invaders to keep the land more peaceful.

Very Important Inventions

Look at this page. Can you say what it is made of? Books are made out of paper. Did you know that the Chinese invented paper? They made it from tree bark, rags, hemp, and old fishing nets! During the Han dynasty, Chinese travelers showed people in other countries how to make paper. Slowly, more and more people learned how to make paper, until even people in Europe knew how to make it. Stop and think. Why was paper such an important invention?

This man is making paper the way the ancient Chinese did, one piece at a time. He lifts a screen out of water mixed with beaten vegetable fibers. The water drains out of the screen and then the fibers dry into a sheet of paper.

During the Han dynasty, a very wise Chinese man called Chang Heng made a machine called a seismograph that told when an earthquake was going to come. Chang Heng's seismograph looks like a statue decorated with dragons and frogs. When an earthquake was going to come, one of the dragons

This is Chang Heng's seismograph. When the earth shakes, a rod inside falls over, causing a dragon to drop a ball from its mouth. The rod falls in the direction the shaking comes from, so the seismograph warns about the earthquake and shows its direction.

would open its mouth and drop a ball into the mouth of one of the frogs! Why is that such an important invention?

The paper dragon is often seen in parades on Chinese holidays. Dover Publications publishes cut-and-assemble paper dragons that fly like paper airplanes. See the Introduction to Geography for Dover's address.

Many Chinese came to our country hoping for better lives. Many of them helped to build the railroads of the West. This was hard work. Did anyone in your family come here then? Or in a friend's family? Could you find out what the work was like?

Vietnam in Ancient Times

If you look on a map, below China on the seacoast east of India you will find Vietnam. It did not have that name in ancient times, but by the time Alexander reached India, people had settled in this land. Being close to China, they learned a lot from the Chinese. But when they began to gather into villages they began to think of themselves as a separate people. For a long time they had grown rice. It was these people who may have taught people in India and China how to grow rice.

Many people in our country today come from Vietnam. Are you from there? Do you have a friend who is?

Introduction to American Civilization

FOR PARENTS AND TEACHERS

Changes are afoot in the teaching of social studies. A public outcry has begun against watered-down social studies textbooks whose chief goal has been to avoid offending anyone—even if that should mean removing all vividness and avoiding fundamental facts of history.

The advisory committees for this series decided to include American history in the very earliest grades. Although some schools now wait until grade five to begin a significant study of American history, our best schools have always started earlier. They have proved that children in early grades are fascinated by stories of the American past—stories that go beyond "Why We Celebrate Thanksgiving."

Perhaps the most important reason for our decision to start early was our concern for fairness. Knowledge of American history and society is gained through the pores by children from advantaged families. It seemed unfair to our committees that children from less advantaged homes are now being denied basic knowledge which helps children understand the social and intellectual world around them. Social and cultural knowledge is built up gradually. An early, systematic exposure to history provides a framework for fuller understanding later on. It is simply unfair that the possession of such a framework should be determined by chance and luck rather than by good schooling.

In Book II we have told stories about high points of American history from our war with Britain, called the War of 1812, to our country's two-hundredth birthday in 1976. Parents and teachers will find suggestions for making the stories more memorable and vivid in activity boxes throughout the chapter.

Good luck in making the teaching and learning of American history great fun!

American Civilization

MORE LEGENDS AND LEADERS

What Happened So Far

Last year we learned about Columbus and Pocahontas, the Pilgrims and George Washington. Do you remember them? You could ask your parents or teacher to read about them again if you don't. We stopped our story shortly after our country's birthday on the Fourth of July, 1776. We had to make a new government based on a constitution, because we said the British King wasn't our leader anymore. Then one of our first presidents, Jefferson, bought so much land from France that our country was suddenly twice as big as it had been at the beginning.

Troubles

It looked as if we were off to a very good start, but there were some big problems nobody knew how to solve. The slaves who had been brought to our country were still not free. Also, many of the Native Americans were being forced to move farther and farther west by new Americans who weren't going to leave a mostly empty country alone! Buying all of that land meant nothing to the Indians who

had lived there for centuries. They believed the land belonged to them, not to France, or Spain, or the new United States. They didn't want to move out, and they didn't want farmers coming in to cut down the forests and scare away the animals they hunted. They were striking back. Some serious troubles lay ahead because of slavery and the Indians.

Against Britain Again

On top of these problems our new country went to war again with Britain. This was called the War of 1812. How could we win a second war with such a strong country? Would we lose our free-dom and become colonies once more?

Britain really did not want a war with us. She had already been fighting France for years. That struggle with France was the reason she made us so angry. She stopped our ships and searched them to keep us from sending supplies to France. She took our sailors and put them in *her* navy to fight against France. Britain even shot cannonballs into our ships.

So, many Americans wanted to make war against Britain. They were called War Hawks. They were angry because the British were giving guns to the Indians. The British thought we'd stay weak if we had to keep fighting the Indians.

Amazing Victories

When the War of 1812 started, the Americans made a big mistake. They tried to take Canada from Britain and failed. But they did keep the British out of the north of our country and won many victories at sea. This was amazing because the British had a huge navy and ours was tiny! One famous ship is called the *Constitution*. It is *still* afloat, docked in Boston Harbor for tourists to see. Although it is not really an iron ship, it is also called *Old Ironsides* because the oak hull survived many cannonballs.

The *Constitution*.

Another Father

James Madison.

The President during this time was James Madison. He is known as the "Father of the Constitution" because he had more to do with writing it than any other person. He was very short, and he was both smart and courageous. He was a friend of President Jefferson, who wanted him to marry a brave lady named Dolley, which he did.

A Hard Choice

When James and Dolley Madison first went to Washington, D.C., to work for President Jefferson, the White House was not finished, the Capitol building was half finished, and the road between them was mud. Later on, when Madison became president, there were more buildings but still lots of mud.

Madison didn't want war. But the War Hawks and the British pushed him into it. Madison was worried about the decision to go to war because many people in Boston and elsewhere in New England were saying terrible things about him. They said he was being paid by France to fight Britain. They were already furious at the money we had paid France earlier for the Louisiana Purchase, and said the land we bought was a desert! Worst of all, they threatened to leave the United States. It was hard to please some people.

A Brave Woman

After Britain defeated France, she had more time and more soldiers to fight us. One of the worst things she did was to burn down the new capital city, including the White House.

Pretend you are visiting with Dolley Madison in the White House when she learns that the British army is coming. She tells you she does not want to run away, and you ask to stay, too. She lets you help her set the table for a late dinner because the President is out trying to help the men defending the city. You know she is worried because there are not nearly enough defenders.

Suddenly, you hear gunfire close by. Dolley Madison looks at you and says calmly, "The British are coming." Then she moves quickly to save as many things as she can. She asks you to gather the silverware. She tells the gardener to take down a famous portrait of George Washington. She herself pulls down two sets of beautiful red velvet curtains. The painting, the silverware, and the curtains go off in a wagon.

Dolley Madison.

Now the gunfire is coming closer. Mrs. Madison turns to you and tells you the time has come to leave. You set out with her for a meeting place the President has arranged across the Potomac River.

Once you are safely across the river, you worry about the President. You hear he has returned to the White House to make sure his wife has gotten away. Then you learn that the commander of the British army is sitting down to Madison's dinner at the White House.

But then a cheer goes up. You see a ferry boat docking on the Virginia shore, across the river from Washington. On it is a small, tired man and his horse. You hear Dolley Madison call "Jemmy," the President's nickname. Tears come to your eyes as you think how brave the President and his wife are. They may not be much taller than you are, but their hearts are great.

Fire

The British have started a fire at every window of the White House with torches. They've burned the Capitol and other public buildings as well. Only two are saved. Three days later they leave, and you return with the Madisons to a heap of ashes.

But private houses are still standing. The Madisons move in with relatives and start over. The President refuses to go to a safer place. He says Congress can meet in the two buildings left standing. You return to your own time knowing the country is in good hands.

Our Country's Song

After burning Washington, the British moved north to Baltimore. This time they were kept out. The battle was fierce. British ships attacked Fort McHenry on the Baltimore harbor with their big guns. An American named Francis Scott Key was afraid they would win.

Key saw the American flag waving above the fort as darkness fell. All night long the guns roared. Key worried that the fort would be captured. But when morning came, the flag still flew! He was so glad that he made up a poem. He had it printed when he returned to Baltimore. Soon people were singing it because they were happy and proud, too. It was called "The Star-Spangled Banner."

This song became our national anthem. Countries have national songs as well as national flags. Have you heard "The Star-Spangled Banner" before a baseball game? A grown-up can teach you the melody, and you can learn the words, even though some of them are unusual. You can find the words and more about this song in the section on music in this book.

Our Flag as Key Saw It

Was the flag that Francis Scott Key saw waving over Fort McHenry the same as our American flag today? Let's look:

Did you know that our flag was changed many times before it became the flag we see today, with its fifty stars and thirteen stripes? Now the thirteen stripes stand for our thirteen original states and the fifty stars for our present number of states. Why do you think our flag changed so many times?

If you like the story about Francis Scott Key and the flag, you might want to read more about them in Peter Spier's book The Star-Spangled Banner *(New York: Doubleday, 1973). You can see pictures of our many flags in this book, too.*

Have you started to learn "The Star-Spangled Banner"? You can get a record of it and other songs of our country from your school or public library.

Dover Publications has two coloring books about this time in our country. The American Sailing Ships Coloring Book *has a picture of the USS* Constitution *("Old Ironsides"). The* Early American Trades Coloring Book *shows how people worked in those days. There are wig makers, glass blowers, hat makers, and nineteen other crafts. Their tools are shown, too. See the Introduction to Geography for Dover's address.*

The War Ends

The British and the United States had already decided to stop the war when one last big battle broke out in the South. It was the Battle of New Orleans. The Americans won, and many, many British soldiers were killed. Why do you think the message the President sent didn't arrive in time to stop the fighting?

The British wanted peace. The Americans did, too. The two countries would never go to war against each other again.

A Few Settlers Move West

Do you remember that President Jefferson got a great bargain in the Louisiana Purchase? He was able to buy so much land that suddenly the country was twice as big.

Americans had been going west since the colonies began. After the Revolution, more and more of them wanted to go west over the Appalachian Mountains. They had heard that in the lands between the mountains and the Mississippi River food grew easily. There were tales about potatoes popping out of the ground. About pumpkins growing so big that a jack-o'-lantern would look like the Man in the Moon! People had seen lakes as big as seas and so

American pioneers moving westward.

Many pioneers lived in homes they made from logs.

many animals they couldn't count them.

After the Louisiana Purchase there was land west of the Mississippi River, too. This land was needed by poor people and by new people coming in from Europe. But the new land was far away when you traveled in a horse-drawn wagon or walked through forests and up mountains.

Boats and Trains

Then, suddenly, everything changed. An artist named Robert Fulton became an engineer and invented a new kind of boat. It was a steamboat, run by a steam engine. It didn't need oars or sails. It needed only burning wood or coal to heat the water to make the steam to run the engine that ran the boat. Steam engines could get you far up and down the river more quickly than ever before.

Then people started dig-
ging canals so canalboats could
get to more and more places.
The Erie Canal was started in
New York State soon after the
War of 1812. Later you could go
by boat from the Atlantic to the
Mississippi. Steam was also
used to make trains move.
Now you had the railroad. The
early railroads were tiny and
slow and covered their pass-
engers with coal smoke. But they could move across the countryside a
lot faster than wagons could.

Robert Fulton's steamboat.

A Storm

Because of the new boats and trains, people seemed to be pouring into the
West. What started out as a sprinkle turned into a thunderstorm. More and
more people came from Europe. Some had been starving there. The United
States grew so fast that John Adams and Jefferson were still alive when the
twenty-fourth state joined the others. (The two presidents died the same day,
July 4, 1826. It was our country's fiftieth birthday. Both were very old and
proud of their country.)

The people moving west were called "pioneers." This was a word from the
army. When an army marched in the old days, a few soldiers called pioneers
went ahead on foot to make paths and roads for the big army that would
follow. That was just what our pioneers did. They went ahead to prepare the
way for the millions of people who would move to the West. Many pioneers
died. Many Native Americans struggled against them, and also died. Other
Indian tribes were forcibly removed from their lands by the government.
Some were sent to "Indian Territory" and not allowed to leave. They were
often hungry there. The new settlers flooded into their lands.

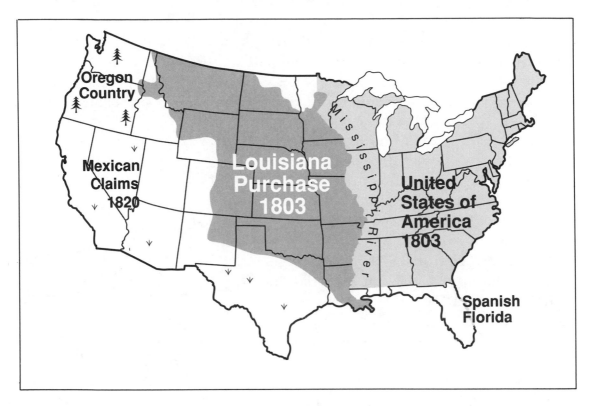

Lone Star State

When you look at your map, you will see that Mexico once held much of the Western part of our country. Some settlers from our country moved into the area that is now Texas. You can find it if you look at the Southern part of our country, almost in the middle.

At first the government of Mexico was glad American settlers moved into the Texas land. There weren't many people there, and the Americans paid taxes to Mexico. But later it seemed too many Americans were coming, and the Mexican Government couldn't stop them.

The Mexican Government had a new President who was strict. The Texans were used to making their own rules. They did not want to be pushed around by the Mexican President any more than the American colonies wanted to be pushed around by the British King. What followed is a bit like what happened between Britain and her American colonies. The Texans decided they wanted to be free of Mexico. Not all of the settlers wanting this were from the United States. Many of the Mexican settlers in Texas agreed.

Remember the Alamo!

Mexico was not going to let Texas go without fighting. Texas had to raise an army quickly and asked the United States Government to help. Texas already had some soldiers. One hundred and eighty-two of them were sent to an old building called the Alamo, a place which had once been a small Mexican church with Spanish priests. Two of these soldiers were famous frontiersmen who had come from the United States to help Texas. You may have heard of Jim Bowie and Davy Crockett. They were at the Alamo.

The battle of the Alamo.

These few men were surprised to see over three thousand Mexican soldiers come to fight them. They thought the Mexican army would wait until spring to come north. By that time, Texas would have more defenders. But the Texans refused to give up, and the Mexicans attacked.

Somehow the men at the Alamo held out through almost two weeks of fighting. The Mexican President said he would kill everyone if the Alamo did not surrender. In the end only five men were left. Jim Bowie even fought from a cot where he had lain sick.

When the Mexican President arrived, he ordered the five male prisoners killed. This was not against the rules of war, but a Mexican general asked to save the men because they had been so brave. The President said "no." If you visit Texas today, you can still see the Alamo.

The Mexican victory did not last long. The Texans were furious about the killing of the five Alamo prisoners and also amazed by the bravery of all of the defenders. They surprised the Mexican army and captured the President. Texas was no longer part of Mexico.

After the Mexican War: Three Times as Big

After a time, Texas was made a state of the United States. But Mexico did not accept this, and made attacks against Texas along the border. The United States Government was angry at the attacks. It seemed that the two countries were headed for war over Texas. But the United States had another reason for going to war against Mexico. It wanted the Mexican lands west of Texas, especially California, where some Americans were already living.

So, neither side tried to keep from going to war. Mexico had a larger army than the United States. But Mexican guns and cannons weren't very good, and the American army was growing quickly. The Americans also had a very clever plan. They took troops by ship to the coast of Mexico, and pushed inland to capture Mexico City. The war was over.

Because of the war with Mexico, the United States grew again, adding the present-day states of California, Nevada, Utah, western Colorado, western New Mexico, and most of Arizona. Remember, Texas had joined the country right before the war.

Now, the United States was more than three times as big as the thirteen original states and stretched from the Atlantic to the Pacific.

Trace the map of the United States and color the new section in a bright color. Do you see how this made the United States three times as big as the thirteen original states? Where do you think the West Coast is? Hint: look for California.

A Dark Time

After the Mexican War, the country stretched from ocean to ocean, but difficult times were ahead. Many people were so against slavery that they did not want the new territories to have slaves. Other people wanted slavery to be stopped everywhere in the country. This conflict led to a war, not against another country like Mexico, but between two groups of states inside our country. It was called the Civil War. Abraham Lincoln was President, and he led the country through the worst time in our history. Many American lives were lost in that war, and you will learn more about it when you study that dark time in a later grade.

Another Kind of Railroad

Even before there was a civil war over slavery, people tried to help the slaves become free, and many slaves tried to escape into freedom. One of the people

A slave family from South Carolina.

who helped slaves escape had been one herself. She was Harriet Tubman, a brave and inspiring leader. At great danger to herself, Harriet Tubman went back to the South many times to lead slaves to freedom.

They traveled over back roads by night and hid by day. They had to be so quiet that babies couldn't even cry. The route Harriet Tubman and others used to help slaves escape was sometimes called the "underground railroad." It wasn't a railroad, and it wasn't underground. "Underground" meant "secret." And "railroad" meant a travel route. The underground railroad meant a secret path to freedom. Along this path many people risked hiding and feeding those making their way to freedom.

After the Civil War, when slavery was ended, Harriet Tubman still didn't

Harriet Tubman.

rest. She made her farm into a home for African-American orphans and ex-slaves.

The Story of Honest Abe

Many people consider Abraham Lincoln one of our greatest presidents.

Abraham Lincoln was born on February 12, 1809 in Kentucky. When he was seven years old, his family moved to Indiana. It was a hard trip through the wilderness because there were no roads.

There is a story that, in Indiana, Lincoln lived for a while in a log cabin that had only three sides. The fourth side was open to the air. It had no door, no window, and no chimney. It did not even have a floor! After a while Lincoln and his father built a better cabin, but it was very plain, too, and life was hard.

Abraham Lincoln.

In Indiana, many of the schoolhouses were very poor. They had fireplaces to warm the children but only dirt floors. There was no glass for the windows. Strips of oiled paper were pasted across the opening instead. There were no desks. Logs were split in half for seats.

Books were very scarce in those days. Most people did not own any, except for a Bible. To do his arithmetic, Abraham used the back of a shovel for a slate to write on, and a burned stick of wood for a pencil. He would do his arithmetic and reading by the light of the fire.

A story is told of how when Lincoln was young, he borrowed a book from a neighbor. The book was about George Washington. Abe read the book until it was time for bed. To keep it safe, he stuck it between two logs of the cabin. One night it rained, and the book was soaked through.

The very next morning Abe took the book back to its owner and said that he had ruined the book. He then offered to pay for it. The man was happy because young Lincoln was so honest. For much of his life Lincoln was known as "Honest Abe."

Young Lincoln never stopped learning, even though he was not able to go to school for long. He studied long and hard on his own and became a lawyer. Soon he was so well known for his honesty and his knowledge of law that he was elected to Congress. In 1860, Honest Abe was elected President.

When Abraham Lincoln was a boy he often read late into the night by firelight.

Last Stand

After the Civil War, there was no holding back the rush of settlers west. Many still went by wagon, but soon the railroad was finished from east to west, and many went by train. Now it was easier to go west. What was going to happen to the Native Americans who were there?

Sitting Bull, head of the Sioux nation.

The same story kept repeating itself. The settlers wanted to farm the Great Plains in the middle of the country. The government was giving the land away to them. Some Indians farmed, too, but many depended also on the great herds of buffalo that roamed the Plains. They saw the farmers killing the buffalo and taking the land. They fought back.

Sitting Bull was the head of the Sioux nation. He and another chief called Crazy Horse called for the Sioux to fight for their land.

The most famous battle was called the Battle of the Little Bighorn. That was the name of the river near the place of battle. General George Custer led a group of United States soldiers who were trying to force the Sioux into a "reservation." They were supposed to accept a stretch of not-very-good land and stay there.

Custer made a mistake and was trapped by a much larger force of Sioux braves. Every last soldier was killed. This defeat is called Custer's Last Stand. But in the end the Sioux were themselves defeated and forced to go to their reservation.

The same thing happened to the Apache tribe in Arizona. They were forcibly removed to a barren reservation. But under a leader named Geronimo large bands of warriors broke out. They said they could not live on such bad land. Geronimo was persuaded to go back to the reservation, but broke out again. So Geronimo and his warriors were sent to jail, and the rest of the Apache were moved to a different reservation. Finally they were all moved to a reservation in Oklahoma where they were carefully watched by soldiers.

Geronimo, an Apache leader.

Wild West Show

To the settlers the West was hard and dangerous. There was a lot of work, bad weather, and Indians who might attack. To the Native Americans the West was practically lost. They were outnumbered by strangers who wanted to farm and ranch. But to people in cities back East the West was thrilling.

Have you ever seen an exciting show like a circus with its acrobats and tightrope walkers? Well, a man named Bill Cody saw that people in the East loved to read what their newspapers wrote about battles with the Indians. Easterners read books that came out about them, too, and wanted more. Bill Cody could see that an exciting show about the Wild West would be very popular. He could sell a lot of tickets as the show moved from city to city.

Cody had worked out West, so he knew what to do. In fact, he was part of the show. He had killed so many buffalo, he was called Buffalo Bill. When the Indian wars were over, he hired Native Americans to dress in their war paint and headdresses. He hired white men to dress as soldiers. Then they would go onstage and pretend to fight for the audience!

There was something else unusual about the show. No one expected to see a woman who could ride and shoot and hunt. But Buffalo Bill hired one of the best shots and one of the best riders in the world—a woman named Annie Oakley.

Annie Oakley.

Dover Publications has a Plains Indian Coloring Book *that accurately describes the costumes and culture of these Native Americans. There are also the following coloring books:* Cowboys of the Old West, Outlaws and Lawmen, *and* Story of the California Gold Rush. *See the Introduction to Geography for Dover's address.*

Children could locate and taste different foods given to the settlers or used by Native Americans: peanuts, corn (including popcorn), chocolate, vanilla, maple syrup, tomatoes, potatoes, squash, pumpkin.

You might like to read Robert Quackenbush's Who's That Girl with the Gun? A Story of Annie Oakley *(New York: Prentice-Hall, 1989).*

The Greatest Lady

In 1876 the United States had its one-hundredth birthday. France, the country that had helped us to be free, gave us a huge statue of Lady Liberty. It must have been the biggest birthday present anyone ever sent! We put the statue on an island in New York Harbor. There all the millions of new people coming from Europe in ships would see it.

These people were mostly very poor so the poem on the statue welcomed them. It says:

> Give me your tired, your poor,
> Your huddled masses yearning to breathe free,
> The wretched refuse of your teeming shore.
> Send these, the homeless, tempest-tost to me,
> I lift my lamp beside the golden door.

Here is the Statue of Liberty on the day it was presented to our ambassador in Paris. Later it was shipped to our country.

Many of these new people stayed in the cities and worked hard in the factories for very little money. Many of their children worked so long they hardly saw the daylight. But there was hope. There was the "golden door." Later on, the workers got together into groups called unions to help them get better pay and healthier working places.

*D*over Publications has a Statue of Liberty Coloring Book. *See the Introduction to Geography for Dover's address.*

Project: Did people in your family or your neighbor's family see the Statue of Liberty when they first came to our country? Can you find out who they were and what their trip was like? They probably cooked the kind of food they were used to in the "old country." Does your family still have a special recipe to share with the class? It might be a German or Polish sausage, an Italian dessert, or any other "ethnic" specialty that children would especially like and could help to make.

Teddy Bear

Have you ever heard of a teddy bear? Of course you have! But you may not know it is named after one of our presidents, Theodore Roosevelt.

Theodore Roosevelt's nickname was "Teddy." The teddy bear got its name because of what happened when Roosevelt was out hunting one time with his friends. They came upon a little bear, but "Teddy" refused to shoot it because it was too small. He knew

Theodore "Teddy" Roosevelt.

that if too many little animals are killed, not enough would grow up to be parents. Soon, that kind of animal could be all gone. When the newspapers found out about this story, they reported it, and soon toy teddy bears were being sold all over the country, and they still are today.

This story shows how worried the President was that our country's plants and animals were being used up. So many new Americans meant whole forests cut down for their houses. Without forests and open spaces, wild animals have no place to live and nothing to eat.

The President had an idea, though. It was to make our national park system really big. He added 250 million acres to it. Little toy bears called "teddy" bears reminded people that the President wanted to save the forests, just as he had saved the little bear when out hunting.

Find a photograph of Yosemite National Park. National Geographic magazine in your library is a good place to look. You will see what wonderful sights our country has. Look especially for photographs of "giant trees" in Yosemite. They are Sequoia trees, named after the Native American who made a written language for the Cherokees. Can you believe these trees were alive as far back as Alexander the Great! See if you can find the famous photograph where a road and an automobile go through one of these giant trees.

Uncle Sam

Have you ever seen someone dressed up to look like "Uncle Sam"? Or have you seen a picture of him? He is very tall, slim, and white-haired and has white chin whiskers. He wears a tall hat and a coat and vest. Most eye-catching of all are his red and white striped pants!

Uncle Sam's name came from the letters *U* and *S*, which is a short way of saying United States. Uncle Sam is a symbol of our country, just as the flag is. He is not really our country's uncle!

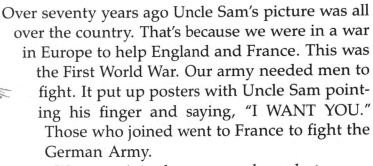

Over seventy years ago Uncle Sam's picture was all over the country. That's because we were in a war in Europe to help England and France. This was the First World War. Our army needed men to fight. It put up posters with Uncle Sam pointing his finger and saying, "I WANT YOU." Those who joined went to France to fight the German Army.

We weren't in the war very long, but everyone else was so worn out we helped to win it. Afterward, our President wanted to start a family of nations so that such a terrible war couldn't happen again. Millions had been killed. But less than twenty-five years passed before an even more terrible war began in Europe again. This was the Second World War. Uncle Sam's picture was up again, saying, "I WANT YOU." The government had not allowed many black men to fight before, but this time everyone was needed. This time our country was in almost the entire war and lost many men, black and white.

Dover Publications has a World War I Uniforms coloring book. See the Introduction to Geography for Dover's address.

Treating Everyone the Same

Even after whites and blacks fought together in the Second World War, African-Americans were still not treated the same as whites. In some places, they could not vote. Many could not ride the same train cars or sit in the same section on buses as white people. They could not eat in the same restaurants. They could not go to the same schools. They could not drink from the same water fountains!

Nine years after the Second World War, in 1954, the United States changed its laws about schools. The new law said that African-American children *could* go to school with white children all over the country. That was one step forward. But in Alabama and other places, whites and blacks still couldn't sit next to each other on buses.

One day, an African-American woman named Rosa Parks got on a bus in the city of Montgomery, Alabama. She was tired because she had worked hard all day. She found a seat and sat down to rest. Soon a white man got on the bus and asked for her seat. Mrs. Parks was very tired and very brave too. She said no, she would not give up her seat to the white man! Because she refused to get up, she was arrested and sent to jail.

A young black minister named Dr. Martin Luther King, Jr., was angry because Mrs. Parks had been arrested. He was angry at the laws which made African-

Rosa Parks.

Americans give up their seats and stand so that white people could sit. It was not fair; black Americans were not being treated equally.

King told African-Americans not to use the buses in Montgomery, Alabama. They would walk or carpool to work or to go shopping. Dr. King said that African-Americans would not ride the buses again until the laws were changed so that they were treated equally. The bus company began to run out of money because not enough people were riding the buses. Soon the laws were changed to give blacks equal rights on buses and trains. Later on, Congress passed stricter laws protecting the rights of all Americans. African-Americans were on their way to having truly equal rights.

Martin Luther King wanted equality for everyone. Today, other leaders are working for changes so that women and all other groups of people will be treated equally. This is called "the Civil Rights Movement." Its purpose is to give everyone in our country a fair chance, and to treat everyone—including children—with fairness and respect.

Dr. Martin Luther King, Jr.

Another Big Birthday

In 1976 our country celebrated its two-hundredth birthday with a party. Tall sailing ships came to American harbors from all over the world—the kinds of sailing ships people would have used to come from Europe to America in 1776. We also gave ourselves a wonderful present. We sent a camera into space to take photographs of the planets. The pictures that have come back show amazing details about the planets.

Before this camera was sent off, we landed human beings on the moon and brought them back to earth—a feat that humans could have hardly imagined in 1776. We placed a small American flag on the moon, the way the old explorers placed their country's flags on new lands. But we didn't claim that the moon belonged to us. We just wanted to leave a visiting card saying that Americans had taken that voyage of adventure. Suppose Alexander the Great could come to the present. Could he believe the beginnings of science in ancient times would turn into something like rockets in space?

Landing humans on the moon was not just an American adventure. Scientists from all over the world contributed to the knowledge that made it possible. The Greeks, Egyptians, Chinese, and other peoples of ancient times contributed when they began to study the world around them and the stars above. Human knowledge about the world has gradually become greater and more accurate, thanks to the work of many scholars and scientists. And the ancient invention of writing has helped scientists of today build on what others have already done. The story of the advance of knowledge is a great story for all humankind, not for any single time or nation.

> Dover Publications has a History of Space Exploration coloring book. See the Introduction to Geography for Dover's address.
>
> Imagine what it would be like to be the first person on the moon! How would you feel if you landed on the moon? Would you need special clothes? Why? Did you know you could jump like a kangaroo if you were standing on the moon? Why?

III.

FINE ARTS

Introduction to the Fine Arts

FOR PARENTS AND TEACHERS

Achild needs to observe and make art in order to understand and appreciate the arts. A book alone cannot adequately convey the experience of music or the impact of visual art. This book *can* hope to provide basic knowledge about art, but parents, teachers, and children themselves must play the main role. Nothing can replace visiting galleries, attending performances, listening to recordings, and encouraging children to sing, paint, sculpt, and playact for themselves.

Although the place of the fine arts in a child's early education is a subject filled with uncertainties and intangibles, civilizations since at least the time of the Greeks have understood that artistic education can have an ennobling effect upon children.

The arts are rightly stressed in many of our elementary schools. Experiences of poetry, music, dance, architecture, and visual arts not only bring joy to children, but also stir and energize their minds with examples of beauty and accomplishment. The development of their artistic sensibilities can enhance the development of their moral sensibilities. It is well understood that stories of good and great actions help instill ideals and values in children. Similar benefits come from children's experience of high achievements in painting, dance, architecture, and sculpture. Today, most schools in the civilized world act upon this principle in their educational policies.

But finally, the value of art in our lives is not just its utility in instilling high ideals in children. Making and appreciating art introduces them to a realm of delight that can last all their lives. Their experiences of the arts can make their lives happier than they would otherwise be.

Fine Arts

MUSIC

The Musical Instruments

We make music when we sing. But there is another way of making music besides using our voices. We can also make music by playing musical instruments like the guitar and piano. There are many different musical instruments and they make many different sounds. Now we'll tell you about some of them.

There is a wonderful piece of music that introduces you to many of the instruments and plays their sounds for you. It is a musical fairy tale called Peter and the Wolf, *by a Russian composer named Prokofiev. There are many recordings of* Peter and the Wolf, *which you can find in record stores and libraries. It is a fun way to learn the sounds of different instruments. And you can act out the parts of Peter and his animal friends.*

Percussion Instruments

You can start playing one kind of musical instrument right away. Maybe you already have. It's called a percussion instrument. It's based on people hitting something like a pot or pan to make a sound. This is called percussion. Percussion instruments include many different kinds of drums. The small

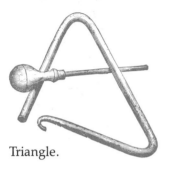

drums make higher sounds, while big drums like the bass drum and the kettledrum make a big low boom! boom! boom! And there are metal percussion instruments that clang when you hit them, like cymbals, bells, and gongs. The main job of percussion instruments is to beat out the rhythm.

Castanet.

Triangle.

Xylophone.

Stringed Instruments

Instruments with strings are called, guess what? You're right! Stringed instruments. There are two types of stringed instruments. The first kind are those you pluck. They include the guitar, the mandolin, and the banjo. The guitar is a plucked instrument that is very popular.

Banjo.

It is used to play folk music, popular music, country music, and even classical music. The harp is also a plucked instrument. It can be as tall as a person or small enough to hold in your lap. Angels in heaven are shown in pictures plucking harps. The harp is one of the oldest stringed instruments in the world.

Plucking a harp.

This is the string section of a symphony orchestra with its conductor.

The second kind of stringed instrument is played with a bow that is drawn over the strings to make them sound. The most common stringed instruments like this are the violin, the viola, the cello, and the bass. The violin is the smallest and makes the highest sounds, and the stringed bass is the largest and makes the lowest sounds. These four stringed instruments—violin, viola, cello, and bass—make up the string section of a symphony orchestra.

Violin.

Wind Instruments

Some instruments you blow your breath into to make sound come out. You can see why they are called "wind instruments." These include the flute, the clarinet, the oboe, and the bassoon. Since these are often made of wood, they are sometimes called "woodwinds." They have a very pleasant, natural sound like the wind blowing through the trees, or like the water of a mountain brook.

Clarinet.

This Sioux Indian flute looks like an elk.

Other wind instruments you blow into are made of brass, like the horn, and these are called brass instruments. They include the trumpet, the trombone, and the tuba. The tuba, which is the biggest, plays the lowest notes. (A note is a single tone, or sound.) Brass instruments often sound bright and shiny, just like the metal they're made of. They're the heart of marching bands and parades.

Tuba.

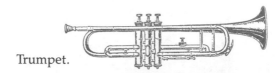

Trumpet.

The saxophone is an instrument which has a sound in between that of instruments like a clarinet and a trombone. It's used frequently in popular music and jazz.

Keyboard Instruments

Some musical instruments like the piano and organ use a keyboard. One person can play many notes at the same time on a keyboard instrument. In fact, you can play as many notes as you have fingers, ten, all at the same time, on a keyboard. The harpsichord is a very old kind of keyboard, while the keyboard processor is a very new one.

Piano.

Electronic Instruments

A very new kind of instrument uses a new way of making sound—electricity! These are called electronic instruments. The electric guitar is one of the most popular. Did you know some computers can be used to make music, too?

You can think of each type of instrument—percussion or wind, for example—as a family. It's fun to learn the sounds each family of instruments makes and to pick them out when you hear music playing.

Understanding and Making Music

Listening to music is a lot of fun, and singing is a lot of fun, too. But did you know you can have even more fun listening and singing if you understand how music works? Do you remember the three parts of music? They are melody, rhythm, and harmony. When you hear someone humming a tune, that's the melody. Now we will tell you how to make a melody by changing the notes, making them higher or lower, louder or softer, and longer or shorter.

A Melody Is a Series of Notes That Go Up and Down

When you sing all of "Row, Row, Row Your Boat" some of the notes go up or down and some stay the same. Try it. "Row, row, row" are all the same, then "your" goes up a little. Then "boat" goes up a little more.

This up and down of the sound of the notes is called pitch. You can remember pitch because in baseball a pitcher pitches the ball higher, way up at the shoulders, or lower, down around the batter's knees. The notes to a song are often like that. Melodies rise and fall, just the way people's voices do when they talk.

Notes are written on a set of lines called a staff, like this:

You can think of the lines of the staff as being like the steps of a ladder. Sometimes the notes go up the ladder, and sometimes they go down, showing you the melody. You sing higher when the notes are high up on the ladder and lower when they are down at the bottom. Sing the beginning of "The Star-Spangled Banner," shown above, trying to follow the notes. You'll see and hear the notes start in the middle on "Oh," and go down the ladder to "say." Then they climb way up the ladder to "see." The printed notes on the staff tell you other things, too. You'll learn more about that in later grades.

Your school or town library has books of songs with the music written in them. You could have fun finding some songs you already know and singing them as you look at the notes for the songs. You'll be able to follow the rise and fall of the melodies you sing, as the notes climb up and down the ladder of the lines.

The Up-and-Down Notes Belong to the Musical Scales

A musical scale is a series of notes going up or down one after another. It is a kind of melody itself. Each note has a name. The names of the notes are: A, B, C, D, E, F, G. You can form many different scales with these notes, depending on which note you start with. One of the most common scales begins with C, and we call it the C major scale. It goes like this: C, D, E, F, G, A, B, C. Let's sing it:

You can play this scale on the piano or other keyboard by playing just the white keys. Begin with the white key just below the two black keys that are together. Like this:

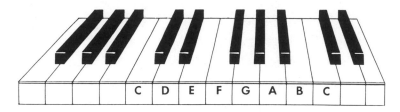

Let's Sing a Song to Learn the C Major Scale

The notes of the C major scale are often called by sounds instead of letters, like this:

do   re   mi   fa   so   la   ti   do
C   D   E   F   G   A   B   C

The song, "Doe, a Deer," can help you learn the scale because it turns the sounds do, re, mi into a story you can remember. Let's sing it:

Do Re Mi

Doe—a deer, a female deer,
Ray—a drop of golden sun,
Me—a name I call myself,
Far—a long, long, way to run,
Sew—a needle pulling thread,
La—a note to follow sew,
Tea—to drink with jam and bread,
That will bring us back to Do, Do, Do.
(repeat)

Did you notice that the song went higher and higher, as we told you? That's because you were going up the scale.

The Scale and the Octave

Notice that the last note of the eight has the same name as the first note, C. This is because it sounds the same, only higher. How can something sound the same, only higher? When you sing, you will hear that it's true. This eighth note is a special note called an "octave." You can remember that because octave sounds like other words that mean eight, like octagon. Once you reach the octave, you begin the scale all over again.

The Notes of a Melody Change Their Length

When you sing, some notes go by very quickly, while others last so long that you almost need to take a breath while you're singing them. This is called the length of a note. In "The Star-Spangled Banner," near the end, when you sing "O'er the land of the free," you hold "free" a long time, longer than the other notes. In "Row, Row, Row Your Boat" you have to sing the notes for "merrily, merrily, merrily," much shorter than the others, so that they can all fit in. Try noticing while you sing the melody, and you'll see. This is what gives a melody its rhythm.

The Notes of a Melody Change Their Loudness

Notes can be loud or soft. Loudness is called volume. Singing notes more or less loudly can make them express how you feel. For a song that is trying to make you feel sad or sleepy, you may want to sing softly. A song that makes you feel like marching or dancing may be sung loudly.

Many songs often get louder as they get to the end, so that they build up to a big finish. When you listen to "The Star-Spangled Banner," for example, notice how the song gets louder toward the end. Songs get louder and softer at different parts. Listen for these changes in volume when you're listening to music.

Now we know most of the things we need to know about the notes that make a melody:

1) how high or low they are: pitch
2) how long or short they are: length
3) how loud or soft they sound: volume.

Next time you listen to a song, listen for volume throughout a song. Play it again and listen for pitch. Play it again and listen for length. You'll see that you know quite a lot about the notes that make a melody. You can notice these different things about a melody as you sing the songs in the next section.

Patriotic Music

The first kind of music we will talk about in this book will be patriotic music, which is music praising our country. Patriotic music expresses our feelings about our country. Our national anthem, "The Star-Spangled Banner," is our most famous patriotic song. You know what a banner is; it's a flag. "The Star-Spangled Banner" is a song about the American flag. But what is a *spangled* banner? Spangles are sparkling bits of shiny metal that are sewn on clothes or other material as decorations. Our flag is sprinkled with bright stars that are like spangles. That's why Francis Scott Key, the author of our national anthem, called our flag the star-spangled banner. Let's sing it again. Notice how you get louder as you come toward the end.

The Star-Spangled Banner

Oh, say, can you see,
By the dawn's early light,
What so proudly we hailed
At the twilight's last gleaming?

Whose broad stripes and bright stars,
Through the perilous fight,
O'er the ramparts we watched
Were so gallantly streaming?
And the rockets' red glare,
The bombs bursting in air,
Gave proof through the night
That our flag was still there.
Oh, say, does that star-spangled banner yet wave
O'er the land of the free
And the home of the brave?

Here's another patriotic song:

America

My country, 'tis of thee,
Sweet land of liberty,
Of thee I sing.
Land where my fathers died,
Land of the pilgrims' pride,
From every mountainside,
Let freedom ring.

Another patriotic song, "This Land Is Your Land," says that America is for everyone, and has a simple melody which everyone can sing easily.

This Land Is Your Land[1]

This land is your land,
This land is my land,
From California
To the New York island,
From the redwood forest
To the Gulf Stream waters;
This land was made for you and me.

1. "This Land Is Your Land," Words and Music by Woody Guthrie. TRO—© Copyright 1956 (renewed) 1958 (renewed) and 1970. Ludlow Music, Inc., New York, NY. Used by Permission.

Patriotic Marches

Bands and soldiers march to a special kind of music on days like the Fourth of July. Because people march to them, these songs are called marches. The most famous composer of marches was an American man named John Philip Sousa. The next time you see a parade coming down Main Street, or watch one on television, you will almost certainly hear a march by John Philip Sousa, like one called "The Stars and Stripes Forever." Marches are usually played on brass instruments, like horns and trombones and tubas, with drums to keep the beat. When you listen to them, listen to the kind of shiny, bright, brassy sound that marches have. Don't they make you feel like marching yourself?

Religious Music

People play music in churches and temples and other holy places as part of their religion. Religious music is some of the oldest music in the world.

Religious songs include hymns, chants, and spirituals. One of the most famous hymns in America comes from the time of the Civil War, over a hundred years ago. It is called the "Battle Hymn of the Republic."

Battle Hymn of the Republic

Mine eyes have seen the glory
Of the coming of the Lord;
He is trampling out the vintage
Where the grapes of wrath are stored;
He hath loos'd the fateful lightning
Of His terrible swift sword,
His truth is marching on.
Glory, glory, Hallelujah!
Glory, glory, Hallelujah!
Glory, glory, Hallelujah!
His truth is marching on.

Spirituals are another kind of religious song. Many spirituals are from African-American churches and are sung during their services. One of the most famous spirituals is called "Swing Low, Sweet Chariot."

Swing Low, Sweet Chariot

Swing low, sweet chariot,
Comin' for to carry me home,
Swing low, sweet chariot,
Comin' for to carry me home.
I looked over Jordan and what did I see
Comin' for to carry me home,
A band of angels comin' after me,
Comin' for to carry me home.
If you get there before I do,
Comin' for to carry me home,
Tell all my friends I'm comin' there too,
Comin' for to carry me home.

Carols are religious songs that are sung outside of church, as well as inside. Some of the most familiar carols are played at Christmas and so are called Christmas carols.

Almost all religions use music because music is one of the best ways to express feelings.

Popular Music

The music that most people like to sing and play today is called popular music. This includes the songs that you hear on the radio, in the movies, and on television. Some of the most popular kinds of music now are rock-and-roll, country, and soul. When you hear music on the radio, which kind do you like best?

The kinds of songs that people like one year may not be popular just a short time later. But some songs are so good that people like to sing them long after they were first written and played. Here is a popular song from earlier times in America that people still like to sing today.

Take Me Out to the Ball Game

Take me out to the ball game.
Take me out to the crowd.
Buy me some peanuts and Cracker Jacks.
I don't care if I never get back,
'Cause it's root, root, root for the home team.
If they don't win it's a shame.
For it's one! two! three strikes you're out!
At the old ball game.

VISUAL ARTS

Art That We Look At

Now we are going to learn about kinds of art that we look at.

What are the different kinds of art that we look at? One kind is flat, and hangs on walls. Can you guess what it is?

It's a picture. Some pictures are called paintings. Paintings are pictures made with paint.

The person who makes one is called a painter. He or she can put the paint on paper, or a wood board, but painters most often put it on a thick cloth called a canvas.

Find a special place to put all the artwork you make. It can be a bulletin board or the refrigerator door for pictures. It can be a shelf for statues. You can make your own art gallery—a place just for artwork!

Another kind of art we look at isn't flat. It stands on the ground or on a table. We can often walk around it and sometimes even touch it. This kind of art is called a sculpture or a statue. Sculptures are often made of stone, wood, or metal. An artist who makes sculptures is called a sculptor. Are there any pictures of sculptures in this book?

Do you know that a building can be a work of art too? The art of planning buildings is named architecture. An artist who plans buildings is called an architect. Is creating buildings an important art? Why?

Are paintings, sculptures, and architecture the only kinds of artwork that we look at? If you said no, you were right! Photography, movies, and craft objects are also works of art that we look at.

Points and Lines in Paintings

Have you ever looked at a work of art and thought about how it was made? Look at this painting, called *Figures in the Night*. It was made by an artist from Spain named Joan Miró. What do you think the two big black blots might be? The artist who made this painting had fun imagining make-believe creatures and painting them. Look closely at the marks Miró has painted between the two creatures. You are going to find out what to call the marks and why they are in this painting.

You may already know some of the most important parts of art, because you are learning about them in math! In the math section of this book, you learn about points and lines. Points and lines are very important in artworks too.

Do you remember that a point is an exact spot? One way to show a point is with a dot like this: (•) Look back at the painting by Miró. Can you see any points?

In math, you learned that a line is straight. In art, lines don't have to be just straight. They can zigzag. They can bend. They can wiggle. They can wander all over the page and cross themselves. When you draw lines on a page you will see that they are usually mainly straight or mainly curved. Find a straight line in the painting by Miró. Find the zigzag line.

You can see that lines do many things in Miró's painting. Let's find out more about lines. Look at these lines.

What do you notice about them? They are straight lines. Do you see that they point in different directions? The lines that point up and down are called vertical lines. The lines that point side to side are horizontal lines. The lines that are leaning are called diagonal lines. In one spot, Miró has painted vertical lines, horizontal lines, and diagonal lines all coming together! Can you find it?

Where is the zigzag line in Miró's painting? Now that you know how to name the lines, can you say what kind of lines make up a zigzag? Draw a horizontal line on a paper. Underneath it, draw a zigzag. Notice how a horizontal line only moves from side to side. Now look at the zigzag. See how a zigzag line moves up and down, and also side to side. You might say that the zigzag is more lively or active compared to a horizontal line because it moves in more directions.

Here are some more lines. How are these lines different from the ones you just looked at? These lines bend. The lines that bend a little are called curved lines. The line that bends all the way around to where it first started is called a circle. The line that keeps curving inside itself is called a spiral. The painting by Miró has lots of bending lines. It also has lines that almost look like circles. Where are they?

Have an older person cut open an orange or a lemon across the segments. Look at the inside. Do you see any straight lines? Do these lines remind you of anything in Miró's painting? What about round lines? After you look at the orange, you can eat it anytime, lines and all!

This picture is not the real painting by Miró. It is a photograph of the real painting. Take a piece of writing paper and fold it in half. That would be about the size of the real painting. Before we look at another painting, here is a funny story about Miró. You will never guess where Miró found the canvas for this painting. He took it from a trash can! If you were looking at the real painting, you would see the edges of the canvas are not straight and neat. They are curvy and rough. Another artist threw the canvas away because it was small and the edges were not perfect. But that is just what Miró liked about it!

> You can make a painting using paper and crayons, or paper and water colors. Have fun imagining stories about make-believe creatures. Then paint them!

More Lines in Paintings

Here is another painting that has lines. It is by an artist named Georgia O'Keeffe. This is a painting of something you may have seen before—a shell. But paintings don't need to be about things we have seen before. Look back at

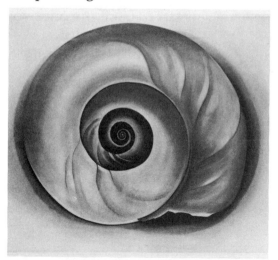

the painting by Miró. Is Miró's painting of anything you have seen before in real life? Paintings can be about pre-tend things or about real things.

O'Keeffe loved things of nature like flowers, shells, and bones. She painted them very carefully, and she often made them much bigger than they really are, so that people could not miss them! For example, the little shell O'Keeffe painted was only an inch or two from side to side, but she painted it the size of a beach ball.

In O'Keeffe's painting, are there any lines? Remember, lines can be straight or curved. You have already learned the name for the kind of line in this painting. It is a spiral. Put your finger on the spiral line and trace the bends it makes. Feel how much your finger moves.

Mass and Line in Sculpture

In this book, we tell you how the Olympic Games started. The Greeks liked all kinds of games, including sports. This statue, called the *Discus Thrower,* is of a Greek person who is trying to throw a discus farther than anyone else. A discus looks like a big Frisbee made out of metal. Find the discus in this picture.

Does this statue look like a real human body? Run your hand over your face and your arm. Can you feel the dips and bumps that your nose, your chin, and your elbow make? Your nose and your elbow stick farther out than the spot under your chin. If you ran your hand over this statue, you would feel that it has dips and bumps too. It's not flat like a picture. Things like chairs and tables—things that aren't flat—are said to have mass. Your body has mass. So does a sculpture.

Let's look at the *Discus Thrower* again. This sculpture not only has mass; it also has lines. Let's see how. Put a thin piece of blank paper over the picture and attach it there with paper clips. You should be able to see the *Discus Thrower* through the blank paper. Draw a straight line from his hand to his chin. Draw another straight line from his chin to his hip. Now a straight line from his hip to his knee. Finally, draw a straight line from his knee to the heel that sticks up in the air. (You can look at the picture here if you need help seeing where to draw your lines.) Now unclip the pages and look at what you drew. A zigzag line! Where else have we seen a zigzag line? You have just learned that even though statues have mass, they also have lines!

Why is the zigzag line important in this statue? Let's look back at the *Discus Thrower.* A discus may look like a Frisbee, but it is much heavier. Hold a big book in one hand, like the *Discus Thrower.* Stand with your knees bent, move your arms to one side of your body and look over your shoulder like the *Discus Thrower.* Can you feel that your body would have to work hard to throw a discus? Do you remember that the zigzag line in Miró's painting shows movement or action? Even though this statue does not move, the zigzag line helps show that throwing a discus takes action.

Mass and Line in Architecture

Some people think that architecture is like a sculpture, but a sculpture that has space inside it and is so big you can walk around in it. In the history section of this book, you can read about one work of architecture, the temple that the Greeks built for the goddess Athena. This temple, the Parthenon, is a splendid work of architecture. Can you see that the Parthenon has mass?

Lines are just as important in the Parthenon as they were in the *Discus Thrower.* Find the steps in the Parthenon. What kind of lines do the steps make? Horizontal lines. Now find the vertical lines. The parts of the parthenon that draw vertical lines are called columns. Do you see that the part of the roof that sits on the columns also makes a horizontal line?

This drawing shows what the Parthenon looked like when it was brand-new. Find the diagonal lines in the roof.

Look at the front of the Parthenon. Imagine there is a vertical line right down the middle of it. Count the number of columns on the right side of your imaginary line. Now count the number of columns on the left side of the line. You will find that there are four columns on each side of the line. When an object is the same on both sides of an imaginary line we say it is "symmetrical." The Parthenon is a symmetrical work of art. You are also symmetrical! Imagine there is a line running from the top of your head to between your feet. You have one eye, and one leg, and one arm on each side of the line.

In the Parthenon, the columns have an important job to do. They hold up the roof. But the columns are important for other reasons. When we look at the columns, we may feel a certain way about the temple. The vertical lines of the columns point in the direction of the sky.

To see why the columns have an upward feeling, try this. Lie flat on the ground. Your body may feel very solid because it presses down into the ground. You are making a horizontal line. Horizontal lines go out in the same direction as the ground, but vertical lines go up toward the sky.

Now stand up straight with your arms reaching to the ceiling. You are making a vertical line. How does standing up with your arms overhead feel compared to lying down? Many people say that horizontal lines in architecture may feel more heavy and solid, while vertical lines seem to have more energy and are lifting up to the sky.

In the Parthenon, we get both the feeling that horizontal lines give to architecture and the feeling that vertical lines give to architecture. The building is full of energy, but it is also very calm. The horizontal and vertical lines balance each other.

A Very Different Building

Here is a very different work of architecture. In the history section of this book, we tell how Buddhism spread through India. This Indian building is a temple for Buddha. It is called the Great Stupa, and it is in Sanchi, India.

Look at this picture and then the picture of the Parthenon. Would you say that the Great Stupa has a lot of straight lines compared to the Parthenon? The Stupa does have lines, but not very many straight lines. If you walked around it, you would walk in a circle. And a line running from one side of the Stupa across the top to the other side would be curved. In fact, it would be half a circle.

If you learned math last year, you may already know about a shape called a sphere. A sphere has the same shape as a ball. The Great Stupa is half a sphere. In architecture, a half sphere like the one on the Stupa is called a dome.

The dome is as important in architecture as straight lines are. When we look at a dome we may feel a different way than we do when we look at straight lines. The outside of a dome may remind us of the shape of hills. The Indians say that when you walk around the Great Stupa, you are walking the Path of Life around the World Mountain.

Open and Closed Buildings

Compare the pictures of the Parthenon and the Great Stupa with the picture of O'Keeffe's shell. Does it look like there are many ways in and out of the shell? Does the shell look like it has an open form or a closed form? Hint: The shell is supposed to close off and protect the creature that lives inside it.

Look at the pictures of the two temples again. See how there seem to be lots of ways to walk in and out of the Parthenon? Do there seem to be many ways to walk in and out of the Great Stupa? The Greeks used lots of columns so that the Parthenon would look like it was open to the air. We say that the Parthenon has an "open form." The Indians did not build many doors in the Great Stupa. They did not make any windows in their temple. The Great Stupa is not very open to the air. We say that the Great Stupa is a "closed form."

It makes sense that the Parthenon is an open building. The Parthenon was supposed to be like a house that the goddess Athena could visit and leave whenever she wanted. The Parthenon should be able to let Athena in and out.

It also makes sense that the Great Stupa should be a closed form. Inside the Great Stupa are little objects that the Indians think belonged to Buddha. The Great Stupa was built to protect those little objects from outsiders. Not many people are supposed to go into the Great Stupa, and none of Buddha's precious objects are supposed to leave the Great Stupa. No wonder people decided to make Buddha's temple a closed building.

In a sandbox, wet the sand a little bit. Pack a round teacup full of sand and turn the teacup over. Carefully take off the teacup. You will have made a dome out of sand! (If you cannot find a round teacup to use, you can also pack the sand together with your hands to make a dome.)

Moving In and Out of Pictures

If you have practiced numbers in the math section of this book, you may already know the number in this picture. It is the number five. This painting is called *I Saw the Figure 5 in Gold*. It is by a man named Charles Demuth. Compare this painting to O'Keeffe's painting. Remember how the spiral line moved in the shell? The Demuth painting is not of anything in nature. But there are a lot of lines moving in this painting too. Find the diagonal lines and see where you think they might be moving.

Is the number five hiding in this painting? No! The number five takes up a lot of room. Also, you can see more than one five. Many diagonal lines seem to be going to or from the number five.

Does the five seem to be running away from you into the painting, or rushing toward you out of the painting? The diagonal lines help make us feel as though the number five could be moving into or out of the painting.

See if you can find other kinds of lines in Demuth's painting. Can you find any curved lines? What about circles? If you hunt carefully, you will also be able to find a spiral.

Learning More About Depth

The artist who made this painting, called *Peasant Wedding*, was named Pieter Bruegel the Elder. A lot is happening in it. People are talking. Some are playing musical instruments. Others are eating. One little girl is sitting by herself with her finger in her mouth. Bruegel made this painting look very crowded and busy with lots of people.

The clothes that the people are wearing do not look like the clothes we wear, because Bruegel painted this many years ago when people dressed differently. But we still do the same kinds of things these people do! Most of them are sitting at a large table. They have all come together at a meal to celebrate a wedding. Can you find the bride in this painting? Here is a hint to help you find her. A special hat is hanging upside down on a hook above the bride's head.

If you look at the Bruegel painting, you may feel as though you could move into it or out of the room where the people are. Now look back at the painting of the number five. It also looks as though there was a space you could move in or out of. But Bruegel doesn't give you this feeling by using diagonal lines. He mainly uses the size of the people to help make you feel as though you could move into or out of the room.

Who are the people closest to you? The men carrying the tray. They seem closest because they are biggest. Have you noticed that things look bigger when they are close? Try bringing your hand slowly up to your eyes, and slowly bring it away. Notice how it looks bigger when it is close and smaller when it is farther away.

The big, close people are in the "foreground" of the painting. The people next in size are in the middle of the room. We say they are in the "middle ground." The people standing in the doorway are the smallest, so they look as though they are in the very back of the room. We say they are in the "background."

The Persian Tale

If you look carefully at this Persian painting by Aqa Mirak, you might feel that it is trying to tell a story. A King sits on his cushion and looks at all the people of his court. One of these men seems to have fallen down. His turban has fallen off and his eyes are closed. There is a rose by his hand. Another man claps his hands.

In fact, Mirak did want this picture to help show a story. He painted it to go in a book. We call this kind of picture an "illustration." The painting is the size of a piece of writing paper. It is called *The Physicians' Duel*. It helps tell the story of one doctor who became the King's favorite by tricking the other doctor with a magic deadly rose.

Compare this painting to the one by Bruegel. Can you see that Aqa Mirak did not make a foreground, middle ground, and background the way that Bruegel did? Bruegel wanted you to feel like you are looking in a window of the wedding hall, or even like you are in the room yourself. But Mirak wanted you to be able to see and enjoy the ducks in the pond, the King's court, the gardens outside, and the traveler with a horse in the distance, even if you could not see all this from one spot in real life.

This photograph makes the painting look like it is in black, white, and gray. But the real painting is filled with very bright colors. This illustration came from a book made for a King. The paints used by the artist cost a lot of money because precious stones, gold, and silver were crushed up and used to make the colors. You must use your imagination to think of what this might look like with colors. Make your own painting using the brightest colors you can. Imagine what could be used to make these colors.

The Importance of Light

We have looked at a lot of paintings so far. Here is a different kind of artwork. Can you tell from the picture what this work of art is? It is a statue of an American hero, Abraham Lincoln. If you have read the history section of this book, you may already know that Abraham Lincoln was President during the American Civil War. He led the country through one of the worst times in our history.

This statue is part of a building called the Lincoln Memorial. The words "memorial" and "memory" start out looking and sounding very much the same. That is because both words have to do with remembering. The Lincoln Memorial was built to help Americans remember Abraham Lincoln. Paintings, statues, or buildings that are built to help people remember the heroes of their nation are called "patriotic art." Can you think of other famous American patriotic art?

You can see that this is a statue of Abraham Lincoln sitting on a chair. The chair is on a big step called a "base." If you were standing next to the base, your head would probably not even reach Lincoln's foot! Abraham Lincoln was tall when he was alive, but he was certainly not this big! The sculptor made him much bigger than he could have been in real life so that people would be sure to notice him. The statue is also big to show that Lincoln was a very important person in our history.

Here is a true story about this statue that teaches how important light is when we look at an artwork. When the sculptor was making the statue, the lights he used shone down from above the statue. Using this light, the sculptor carefully made the statue's face look as though Abraham Lincoln was thinking deeply. The little picture here shows how he wanted Lincoln to look.

But when the statue was moved into the Lincoln Memorial, light from the sun came up at the statue from the open door. The next picture shows how Lincoln looked when sunlight shone through the open door. Instead of looking thoughtful, Lincoln looked surprised!

The way sunlight shone on the statue had completely changed the way Lincoln's face looked. In order to make the statue look the way it should, electric lights were put inside the Lincoln Memorial so that light would shine down strongly from above the statue. With electric lights, Abraham Lincoln's face looked as the sculptor thought it should.

This story tells us something very important about light and artwork. Artists know that the way light falls affects the way things look to us. That is because of the way that shadows are made when light shines on things. Light on one side of a thing makes a shadow on the opposite side. The way light and shadow fall can make us pay more attention to some things and less attention to other things.

Find a partner. Now get a flashlight. Turn out the lights in the room so that the only light comes from the flashlight. Put the light below your partner's chin so that it shines up on your partner's face. Now put the light above your partner's head so that it shines down on your partner's face. See how the shadows change and make your partner's face seem to change? Shine the light from all different sides. See what kind of shadows light makes, and how it makes your partner's face look. (If you don't have a partner, you can become your own partner! Just shine the light on your own face as you look in the bathroom mirror.)

Light and Lines Help Us Pay Attention

This painting is by a man named Jan Vermeer. For Vermeer, light was one of the most important parts of a painting. In this painting, what does the light shine on? Which direction is the light coming from?

This painting is not of a famous person. The name of the painting, *Woman with a Water Jug*, doesn't even tell us who she is. Her clothes do not have fancy designs, so she is probably not rich. She is not even doing anything out of the ordinary. Even though this woman is not famous or rich, the way Vermeer paints her makes her seem special and makes it easy for us to remember her.

The vertical and horizontal lines of the window and table make us pay more attention to the places where the light falls most strongly. As you can see, Vermeer used both these lines and strong light to help us pay close attention to the woman. These make her seem special.

What Have You Learned?

You have learned a lot in this section! You found out that art you look at can be in the form of paintings, sculptures, or architecture. You learned that artwork can be about real or imaginary things. You learned to see lines in artwork. You found out about mass in sculpture and architecture. You have learned about depth in paintings. And you have seen how important light is for artwork. See if you can find these things in works of art you haven't seen before.

Get some magazines or newspapers that you are allowed to cut from. Find works of art in these and cut them out. Glue or tape these pictures onto blank pieces of paper. When you have filled many pieces of paper with artwork, staple the pieces of paper together at one corner. Now, whenever you want to enjoy some works of art, you can look at your own artbook!

Understanding and Making Drama

What is Drama?

You remember that drama is play-acting. When you play with dolls, you are doing drama. When you talk to them or pretend that one of them is your friend, and give them words to say, that is drama. When you play cops and robbers, you are also acting out a drama. When you pretend that you are the cop who catches the robber in a bank, you are performing a kind of play. Television and movie plays are drama. Years ago, for our ancestors, drama played out on the stage with live actors was as common as television and movies are for us today.

Drama in Early Times

People have been play-acting for thousands of years throughout the world. Some Native American and African people acted out the hunting of wild animals before or after the hunt. In ancient Greece, over two thousand years ago, people used to perform plays out-of-doors before huge crowds. People would sit on the great rounded steps of stones placed on hillsides to watch the plays. These places were called amphitheaters.

These Native-American children are dancing in a traditional tribal dance.

This is where European drama began, and we still read and perform many of the ancient Greek plays today. The Greek actors wore masks and costumes to help them pretend to be the characters they were portraying, just as you might wear a mask and costume on Halloween in order to pretend to be a monster or a knight. Today people usually wear costumes and makeup when they act.

Drama gradually moved indoors, into theaters, which is where you can see most plays today. Theaters have a stage where the actors perform and a place for the audience to sit, which is kept dark the way it is in a movie theater. They have bright lights that shine on the stage and places where the scenery can go behind or above the stage when the scenes are changed.

Here is an amphitheater.

Comedy and Tragedy

Just to remind you, there are two major kinds of drama, comedy and tragedy.

Comedies are plays that are funny and make you laugh. They show how foolish people can be, and how funny the world sometimes seems. They make you feel good, because they make you smile at your difficulties. People like comedies a lot. They have for over two thousand years! Today, many television shows and movies as well as plays are comedies. The symbol of comedy is a mask of someone smiling. Can you find it on this page?

One kind of comedy that began in America is called musical comedy. In a musical comedy, people sing and dance as well as act. Many popular songs were written for musical comedies.

Tragedies are just the opposite of comedies. They are plays about very sad things, and they can even make you cry. But in a way they make you feel better, too, just as you feel better sometimes when you've had a good cry. They tell you that other people understand when things are sad, and that you are not alone. The ancient Greeks wrote some of the greatest tragedies. The symbol of tragedy is the mask of someone crying. Can you find it opposite the mask of comedy?

Plays are divided into different sections called acts, and acts are divided into still smaller sections called scenes. The men and women who act in plays are called actors, and the people they are pretending to be are called the cast of characters. A person who writes plays is called a playwright.

Performing Your Own Drama

Drama is not only fun to watch, but also to perform. Here is a play that you and your friends can act out.

It is the story of "Anansi Rides Tiger." You might have read this story in the first book of this series. Now we are going to present it as a play, so that you can act it out. One of the fun things about acting out "Anansi Rides Tiger" is that you can pretend to be different kinds of animals.

The set is another word for the scenery, and shows you where a play takes place. The words of a play are called the script. In a script, you don't say the words that are printed between parentheses and in italics *(like this).* They tell you where to move and are called stage directions. You do say the other words that are printed below or after your character's name. They are called your lines. Here is the script for *Anansi Rides Tiger:*

NOTE TO PARENTS AND TEACHERS: One of the reasons we chose this play is so those in it can have the fun of playing animals. Most of the animals do not have any lines, except as a kind of chorus, so the play can be done with as few as three or four people, or as many as you'd like. You can easily make the roles of the chorus animals larger, simply by having them react in their different ways to what's going on between Anansi and Tiger, etc.

You can do the play as simply or as elaborately as you'd like. You can simply read it out loud, or act it out in class or your living room. Or you can mount an actual production (we've given stage directions), with a set, costumes, etc.

Anansi Rides Tiger

CAST OF CHARACTERS

BRER TIGER: Tiger is very fierce and strong. When he's angry, he's very angry and opens his mouth very wide and shows his teeth. He likes to threaten other animals by growling.

ANANSI: Anansi is a spider. He should move as if he's afraid of being eaten, always looking about to see where the tiger and other animals are. But he's also very clever and sly.

LINDA: Linda may be an elegant and beautiful girl, but she's also very stuck-up.

THE NARRATOR: The narrator must speak very clearly.

THE ANIMALS: Snake, Bear, Elephant, Owl or any animals you want to be.

SETTING:

A jungle. On one side of the stage, or brought on later, is Anansi's hut.

(Curtain opens on set of jungle forest. Narrator comes out on stage, and addresses audience)

NARRATOR: Hello. Tonight we are going to perform for you the story of "Anansi Rides Tiger." This story takes place in the deep forest. The forest is filled with many animals. There is Snake,

(SNAKE comes onto stage, slithering as he walks)
Owl,
(OWL flies onto stage, lands, wipes his eyes as if just waking up)
Elephant,
(ELEPHANT comes onstage; NARRATOR names other animals [if wanted] that come onstage as she names them)
———, ———, and Bear.

(BEAR lumbers onto stage last)

Now bears, as you've probably heard, are pretty fierce.

(Other ANIMALS make way for BEAR)

But the fiercest animal of the whole forest was Brer Tiger.

(Big roar from TIGER offstage. All the ANIMALS jump and move away from roar)

All the animals were afraid of Tiger.

But the one who was most afraid of him

(*There is another roar from offstage, and* ANANSI *runs onstage, afraid*)

> was Anansi, the spider. Anansi thought the world of himself,

(ANANSI *looks out at audience, smiles and takes a bow. There is another growl, and* ANANSI *cowers and hides behind the other animals*)

> but he was just a puny spider after all.

(BRER TIGER *growls and comes onto stage. Other* ANIMALS *shy away from him in fear. He turns and growls and raises his paw at them, and they back away even further.* TIGER *struts around, very proud.* ANANSI *comes out, and struts like* TIGER, *making fun of him, without* TIGER *seeing him. All the* ANIMALS *laugh.* TIGER *looks around, and* ANANSI *hides behind* ANIMALS. TIGER *struts away again.* ANANSI *whispers something to other* ANIMALS *and they all laugh.* TIGER *comes toward them and they all run offstage in fear*)

> Yes, all the animals in the forest were afraid of Tiger. But there was one creature that even Tiger bowed down to. That was . . .

(LINDA *comes out onstage, she has a mirror, and admires herself in mirror, etc.*)

> Linda, the most beautiful girl in the forest.

(TIGER *bows to her, and his growl turns into a meow*)

> Tiger loved Linda and wanted to marry her. But here's the thing.

(NARRATOR *whispers to audience*)

> So did Anansi, the spider.

(*Normal voice*)

> Now Tiger was especially fierce, because this was the day that Tiger was going to ask Linda to . . .

(TIGER *takes out ring, clears throat*)

TIGER: Marry me.

LINDA: (*Laughs*)
            Marry you? Why should I marry you?

TIGER: But, why not?

LINDA: Anansi, that puny spider, says you're not so fierce. He says you're his riding horse, and he's your master. You're not a fierce tiger, at all.

TIGER: What? His riding horse? I'm his riding horse?
            (*All the* ANIMALS *laugh*)
            That puny . . . I'm not his riding horse.

LINDA: Oh, really?
            (*Fixes her hair*)
            Prove it.

TIGER: (*Lets out a roar.* ANIMALS *cower. Lets out another roar as he runs offstage*)
            Anansi!

NARRATOR: Tiger was off to find Anansi, whom he never much liked anyway.

(*We hear* TIGER *calling out,* "ANANSI," *and growling, offstage.* ANANSI *creeps onto stage, and slips under the covers of his bed.* TIGER *bounds onto stage. Stands outside hut area*)

TIGER: (*Growling*)
            Anansi, come out here. Anansi!

ANANSI: (*Pulls the covers down, just below his eyes. Very sickly:*)
            This is Anansi.

TIGER: Come out here!

ANANSI: Tiger, I have a fever. I'm too weak to move. I'm near death.

TIGER: (*Bounds into hut*)
            That's the truth. Linda thinks I'm your riding horse.

ANANSI:	Where did she get that idea?
TIGER:	From you. You have to tell her I'm not your riding horse.
ANANSI:	Can't she see that for herself? Oh, please, I feel so faint. Please let me die in peace.
TIGER:	Not until you tell her about me.
ANANSI:	I'd like to—but I feel so faint. Maybe you could carry me.
TIGER:	Oh, very well. Get on.
ANANSI:	And I'll need a fly swatter so those jungle bugs don't eat me alive. I'm so frail.
TIGER:	Oh, very well. (*Exits, brings back a branch*) Here. Now get on.
ANANSI:	Maybe you should give me the ring you got for Linda. You might lose it.
TIGER:	Yes, good idea. (*Gives him ring*) Now, get on. (ANANSI *gets on, piggyback style, holding fly swatter. They exit. Other* ANIMALS *enter onto stage*)
NARRATOR:	And so it was that when Linda and the animals caught sight of them . . .
BEAR:	Look! Look! (BEAR *and other* ANIMALS *look and laugh, cackle, etc.* ANANSI *and* TIGER *enter,* ANANSI *riding* TIGER)
NARRATOR:	they saw Anansi riding Tiger, just as he'd said.
ANANSI:	See, Linda, what did I tell you? I can ride Tiger anytime.
LINDA:	It does look that way.

TIGER: What?

ANANSI: Tiger gave me his ring. Please accept this as a token of my regard.

LINDA: I am honored.

TIGER: But, Linda . . . I . . .
              (*Turns his head toward* ANANSI, *who's riding him*)
              You!
              (*Roars and growls*)

ANANSI: (*Slaps him with tree branch*)
              Giddyup, Tiger! Giddyup!
              (TIGER *tries to buck him off, but can't.* TIGER *runs off embarrassed, with* ANANSI *riding him, as* ANIMALS *laugh, cackle, hoot, etc.*)

NARRATOR: Poor Tiger was so embarrassed he hid deep in the jungle forest, never to see Linda again. And that is how Anansi rode Tiger.

              (*Blackout. Curtain.*)

IV.

MATHEMATICS

Introduction to Mathematics, Grades One Through Six

FOR PARENTS AND TEACHERS

Americans do not pay enough attention to mathematics in the early grades. As a proportion of total class time, we spend less time on mathematics and more time on language arts than other countries do. Yet those other countries outshine us not only in math, but also in language arts. Their children's reading and writing levels are as high as or higher than ours by seventh grade. Do they know something we don't know? Yes, and we must change our ways.

It is almost impossible for children *not* to practice the use of language. Their out-of-school practice in speaking and listening helps their performance in reading and writing, since there's a lot of overlap between listening, talking, reading, and writing. But, with so little time spent on math, it is all too easy for children to neglect practicing mathematics, which is a kind of language. Just as English should become second nature to our children, so should math.

The three cardinal principles of early mathematics education are 1) practice, 2) practice, and 3) practice—not mindless, repetitive practice, needless to say, but thoughtful and varied practice. We know that these three principles are the true ones, because they hold for learning in *all* subjects. Well-meaning persons who are concerned to protect the joy of the childhood years wrongly fear that applying these three principles to mathematics portends a soul-killing approach to schooling.

Nothing could be further from the truth. The destroyer of joy in mathematics is not practice but anxiety—anxiety that one is mathematically stupid, that one does not have that special numerical talent. But math talent is no more rare than language talent. The number of great mathematicians and the number of great poets per million of population are roughly similar. Yet people experience math anxiety to a much greater degree than language anxiety, because their early training has denied them systematic familiarity with the vocabulary, grammar, and spelling of mathematics. Those of us who experience math anxiety must resolve not to inflict this educational wound upon our children.

The basic operations of math must be familiar before the principles behind those operations are well understood. Again, an analogy with language learning is pertinent. Most people agree that it's important to learn the alphabet at an early age, before one understands the full significance of the alphabet. Being instantaneously familiar with the sums and differences of any two digits is even more basic than knowing the alphabet. Such knowledge is on a par with knowing basic sentences of English—which is a stage prior to knowing the alphabet.

While practice is the watchword of math, intelligent, fun practice is the hallmark of good math teaching. One teaching hint is worth remembering at all levels of math. Children should be encouraged to practice the same operation or types of problems from several different angles. This is a highly useful way to begin to grasp the relationships behind math operations.

Since intelligent practice and problem-solving activities are essential to learning math, **it is very important to note that the math section of this book must be regarded as a supplement, not as a sufficient vehicle for teaching mathematics.** The section is, in effect, a detailed *summary* of the math that should be mastered in this grade. We have thought it important to include these summaries to help parents and teachers ascertain that children have in fact learned the math they should know in each grade. The math sections must be used in conjunction with imaginative problems and activities taken from workbooks, from standard math texts, or from the imaginations of teachers and parents.

Familiarity through practice in the early grades is a sure road to making mathematics fun, and it's the only road to conquering fear and anxiety in mathematics. Those who follow this very basic teaching principle in early grades will win the gratitude of their children in later years.

Introduction to Second-Grade Mathematics

FOR PARENTS AND TEACHERS

During second grade, students should add a good deal to the knowledge of mathematics they acquired in first grade. By the end of the year, they should have memorized all of the basic addition and subtraction facts, and have learned how to add and subtract three-digit numbers. They should also have begun to memorize the multiplication tables, and have had practice on such important topics as word problems, geometry, fractions, and money.

Learning this material requires consistent effort and practice, but it is definitely within the reach of all students. Those countries that are more successful at teaching mathematics than we are in this country have two things in common: they make a decision about what mathematics students will learn in each grade; and then, to ensure that students learn it, they give all students a lot of practice at it, making some of the practice quite challenging. Thus in each new grade students are ready to learn new material, having mastered the material from the grade before.

It is particularly important that, on each level, challenging questions be a regular part of the curriculum for all students. Part of the reason students in the United States do so badly on complex problems involving a series of steps is that they are not regularly expected to solve them, while their counterparts in other countries are, from first grade on. Also, to answer challenging problems, students must acquire a secure understanding of the mathematics involved in the problems. This secure knowledge greatly benefits them in later grades, when they will have to rely on it as a basis for understanding new mathematics. On the other hand, nothing makes mathematics more confusing than having a vague and unreliable knowledge of what one is already supposed to know. The most common lament of math teachers runs something like this: "How can I teach my students algebra when they don't understand fractions or arithmetic!"

It is important, therefore, that each student learn the material in this second-grade curriculum well before going on to the third grade. For example, students' knowledge of addition and subtraction facts should be quick and accurate. They should regularly rewrite two-digit and three-digit addition and subtraction problems to check them. They should be able to write a multiplication problem as repeated addition, and recite the first few multiplication tables. In general, they should acquire a secure and accurate knowledge of the mathematics in this section, rather than simply a general acquaintance with it. With much (and regular!) practice, students will be well prepared for mathematics in the third grade, and beyond.

Second-Grade Mathematics

Numbers to 100

Skip-Counting, Counting by Twos and Threes

In first grade you learned to count by tens and by fives. Counting by tens or fives is called skip-counting, because you skip over numbers when you count this way. For example, when you count by tens, you skip over all the numbers that come between 10 and 20.

You should also learn to skip-count by twos and threes. To count by twos, count the second number each time, like this:

1, **2,** 3, **4,** 5, **6,** 7, **8,** 9, **10,** 11, **12.**

So to count by twos, you count 2, 4, 6, 8, 10, 12, and so on. To count by threes, count the third number each time, like this:

1, 2, **3,** 4, 5, **6,** 7, 8, **9,** 10, 11, **12,** 13, 14, **15,** 16, 17, **18.**

So to count by threes, you count 3, 6, 9, 12, 15, 18, and so on.

Even Numbers and Odd Numbers

When you count by twos beginning with 0, you are naming the even numbers. The even numbers up to 30 are:

0, 2, 4, 6, 8, 10, 12, 14, 16, 18, 20, 22, 24, 26, 28, 30.

When you count by twos beginning with 1, you are naming the odd numbers. The odd numbers up to 30 are:

1, 3, 5, 7, 9, 11, 13, 15, 17, 19, 21, 23, 25, 27, 29.

Even numbers have 0, 2, 4, 6, or 8 in the ones' place. Odd numbers have 1, 3, 5, 7, or 9 in the ones' place.

Between

In counting, when a number comes in the middle of two other numbers, we say it is between them. For example, 7 is between 6 and 8. We count 6, 7, 8. What numbers are between 5 and 9? 6, 7, and 8 because we count 5, 6, 7, 8, 9.

Number Words from Eleven to One Hundred

Learn to write the number words from eleven to twenty: eleven, twelve, thirteen, fourteen, fifteen, sixteen, seventeen, eighteen, nineteen, twenty. Practice writing these words in order until you can do it easily. Learn to write the number words for the tens: ten, twenty, thirty, forty, fifty, sixty, seventy, eighty, ninety. Practice writing these words until you can write them easily. Also learn the number word for 100: one hundred.

When you know these words, you can write out any number up to 100. Learn how to write out the numbers after 20 that come between the tens. 21 is written out twenty-one. 25 is written out twenty-five. 83 is written out eighty-three.

Addition and Subtraction Facts to 18

Addends

$5+3=8$ 5 and 3 are addends.

Numbers that are added together are called addends. In $5+3=8$, 5 and 3 are addends. Remember that in $5+3=8$, 8 is called the sum. There can be more than two addends. In $2+3+5=10$, 2, 3, and 5 are all addends.

Equations

An equation compares numbers using an equals sign. $3+2=5$ is an equation. $10-6=4$ is also an equation. Remember that the equals sign means "is the same as." $36=36$ is an equation, and so is $4+1=9-4$. All number statements that use an equals sign are equations.

Number Line

This is a number line. A number line shows the numbers in order. A number line has arrows because it keeps on going forever: the picture shows only part of a whole number line. All the numbers you have learned, and many more numbers, can be shown on a number line.

You can use a number line to practice addition and subtraction. For example, to find the sum of $7+4$ on a number line, first go forward 7 numbers, to the 7. Then go forward 4 more numbers. You end on 11. So $7+4=11$.

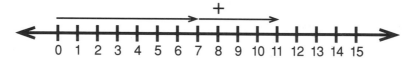

You did the same thing when you counted forward to do addition: $7\rightarrow8$, 9, 10, 11.

You can also use a number line to practice subtraction. Remember that in the equation $10-4=6$, 6 is called the difference. Find the difference of $8-5$, using a number line. First go forward 8 numbers to the 8. Then, because you are subtracting, go backward 5 numbers. You end on 3. So the difference of $8-5$ is 3.

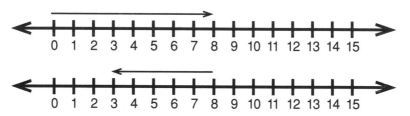

You did the same thing when you counted backward to do subtraction: $8\rightarrow7$, 6, 5, 4, 3.

Addition Facts with Sums of 13, 14, 15, 16, 17, and 18

In first grade you learned all the addition facts with sums up to 12. Here are all the other addition facts. Learn these new facts by heart, so that you can give the sums quickly without stopping to count. You need to practice these new facts especially hard.

Sum of 13	Sum of 14	Sum of 15	Sum of 16	Sum of 17	Sum of 18
$9+4=13$	$9+5=14$	$9+6=15$	$9+7=16$	$9+8=17$	$9+9=18$
$8+5=13$	$8+6=14$	$8+7=15$	$8+8=16$	$8+9=17$	
$7+6=13$	$7+7=14$	$7+8=15$	$7+9=16$		
$6+7=13$	$6+8=14$	$6+9=15$			
$5+8=13$	$5+9=14$				
$4+9=13$					

Notice that none of the addends in the addition facts is greater than 9. That is because if you know how to add together the digits 0 through 9, you can solve $12+4$ like this:

2 ones + 4 ones = 6 ones

one 10 more makes 1 ten 6 ones or 16

$$\begin{array}{r} 12 \\ +\ 4 \\ \hline 16 \end{array}$$

When you know all the addition facts, you will be able to solve any addition problem quickly and easily.

A Table of the Addition Facts

Practice completing a table like this, which shows all of the addition facts. In each box, add together the number from the side and the number from the top. Write down only the sum.

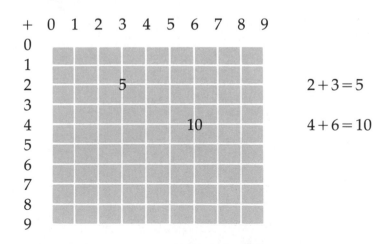

$2+3=5$

$4+6=10$

Subtraction Facts from 13, 14, 15, 16, 17, and 18

In the first grade you learned all the subtraction facts from numbers up to 12. Here are all the other subtraction facts. When you have learned all the subtraction facts, you will be able to solve any subtraction problem quickly and easily.

From 13	From 14	From 15	From 16	From 17	From 18
$13-4=9$	$14-5=9$	$15-6=9$	$16-7=9$	$17-8=9$	$18-9=9$
$13-5=8$	$14-6=8$	$15-7=8$	$16-8=8$	$17-9=8$	
$13-6=7$	$14-7=7$	$15-8=7$	$16-9=7$		
$13-7=6$	$14-8=6$	$15-9=6$			
$13-8=5$	$14-9=5$				
$13-9=4$					

Adding in Any Order, Adding Three Numbers

It does not matter what order you add numbers in, the sum is still the same.

$$9+4=13 \quad \text{and} \quad 4+9=13$$

That is why you can add numbers in a different order to check the work you have done.

When you are adding three numbers, first add down, like this:

$$
\begin{array}{cc}
4 & 7 \\
3 & \\
+\ 5 & +\ 5 \\
\hline
12 & 12
\end{array}
$$

Then check by adding up, like this:

$$
\begin{array}{cc}
4 & 4 \\
3 & 8 \\
+\ 5 & \\
\hline
12 & 12
\end{array}
$$

You should always get the same sum.

Doubling Numbers

Adding a number to itself is called doubling the number. When you add 2 and 2, you double 2. $2+2=4$, so double 2 is 4. Another way to say this is that twice 2 is 4.

Learn all the doubles for the numbers 1 through 9.

$$1+1=2 \qquad 4+4=8 \qquad 7+7=14$$
$$2+2=4 \qquad 5+5=10 \qquad 8+8=16$$
$$3+3=6 \qquad 6+6=12 \qquad 9+9=18$$

Doubles can also help you learn addition facts by heart. If you know $7+7=14$, then you know $8+7=15$. Eight is one more than 7, so $8+7$ must be one more than $7+7$.

Dividing Numbers in Half

When a number is divided into two equal parts, each part is half. 9 is half of 18, because 9 and 9 make 18.

$$9+9=18$$

7 is half of 14, because $7+7=14$. Half means the same thing as one half. What is half of 16? 8, because $8+8=16$.

Dozen and Half Dozen

A dozen is a group of 12. For example, 12 eggs are a dozen eggs. A half dozen is a group of 6. Remember that 6 is half of 12. That is why a half dozen is 6.

A dozen = 12

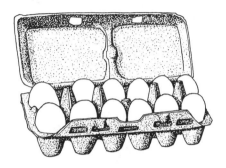

A DOZEN EGGS

A half dozen = 6

A HALF DOZEN STARS

Checking Addition and Subtraction

Because addition is the opposite of subtraction, you can always check subtraction by doing addition.

To check   add like this:

17	8	8
− 9	+ 9	+ 9
8		17 ✓

When you check, you should end up with the same number you began with. You subtracted from 17, and when you add 8 and 9, you get 17. So the problem checks.

You can also check addition by doing subtraction. Here is one example.

To check   subtract like this:

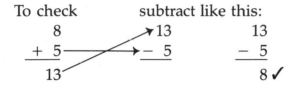

8	13	13
+ 5	− 5	− 5
13		8 ✓

Fact Families

In first grade, you learned to form fact families, given one fact from the family. For example, the fact family for $9+4=13$ also has $13-4=9$, $4+9=13$, and $13-9=4$. Learn to form fact families with the new addition and subtraction facts.

Also notice how finding opposite facts in fact families is the same as checking addition by subtraction and subtraction by addition. Here are two examples.

$$9+7=16 \qquad\qquad 13-8=5$$
$$16-7=9 \qquad\qquad 5+8=13$$

Greater Than and Less Than

Remember that the sign > means greater than.
For example, $10 > 8$; also $7 + 6 > 5 + 6$.

Remember that the sign < means less than.
For example, $23 < 72$; also $15 - 8 < 11$.

Missing Addends

Practice addition facts with one of the addends missing, instead of the sum.

Solve: $7 + \underline{\quad} = 15$ $7 + \underline{8} = 15$

Also practice subtraction facts in the same way.

Solve: $\underline{\quad} - 6 = 7$ $\underline{13} - 6 = 7$

When you can answer questions like these easily, you know your addition and subtraction facts very well.

Questions like this can also be asked with greater than and less than. With less than and greater than, there is usually more than one correct answer.

For example, $15 - \underline{\quad} > 11$

If you put 0, 1, 2, or 3 in the blank, your answer would be correct.

Two-Digit Addition and Subtraction

Regrouping

Remember that 1 ten is the same as 10 ones:

1 **TEN** = 10 **ONES**

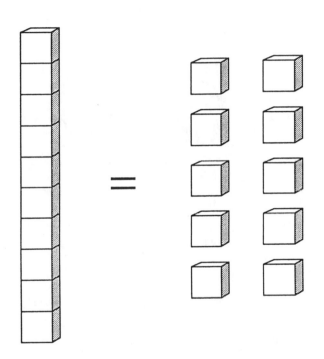

Sometimes when you add, you need to make 10 ones into 1 ten. Making 10 ones into 1 ten is called regrouping. Learn how to regroup.

$$8 + 7 = 15$$

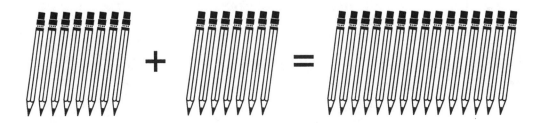

When you add 8 pencils and 7 pencils, you have 15 pencils in all. You can take 10 of the pencils and make them into 1 ten.

15 ones = 1 ten and 5 ones

You have 5 ones left over. So 15 ones is the same as 1 ten and 5 ones.

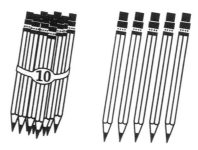

Practice regrouping with addition facts that have sums of 10 or more. Use pencils to show an addition fact. Then show the sum as a group of ten and the ones that are left. Also write the sums of the addition facts as tens and ones, like this:

	tens	ones
		7
+		5
	1	2

	tens	ones
		8
+		9
	1	7

Writing Two-Digit Numbers in Different Ways

Practice writing two-digit numbers in different ways: 77 is 7 tens and 7 ones. 5 tens and 3 ones = 53

64 is 6 tens and 4 ones. 6 tens are the same as 60, and 4 ones are the same as 4. So 64 can also be written 60 + 4. You should be able to write two-digit numbers as a sum, like this: 46 is 40 + 6. 30 + 7 is 37.

Two-Digit Addition

Remember that to add two-digit numbers, first you add the ones. Then you add the tens.

Find the sum.   Add the ones.   Add the tens.
tens ones   tens ones   tens ones
  2   3   2   3   ones'   tens'   2   3
+ 3   5   + 3   5   column   column + 3   5
                   8   5   8

The numbers in the ones' place are called the ones' column. The numbers in the tens' place are called the tens' column. The sum is 58.

Two-Digit Addition with Regrouping

When you add two-digit numbers, sometimes you have to regroup.

Find the sum.

tens ones
  4   8
+ 2   6

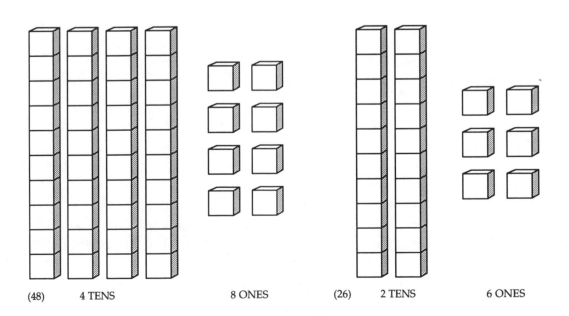

(48)   4 TENS   8 ONES   (26)   2 TENS   6 ONES

8 + 6 is 14 ones. You regroup 14 ones as 1 ten and 4 ones. You write the 4 ones at the bottom of the ones' column. That is how many ones you have. You write the 1 ten at the top of the tens' column. Then you add it to the other tens.

Add the ones. Regroup.	Add the tens.

```
    tens ones                    tens ones
     1                            1
     4    8                       4    8
  +  2    6                    +  2    6
  ─────────                    ─────────
          4                       7    4
```

1 ten + 4 tens + 2 tens is 7 tens. Altogether you have 7 tens and 4 ones, or 74. The sum is 74.

Writing a new ten at the top of the tens' column is called carrying. For example, in the last problem someone might say "carry the one" while writing the 1 at the top of the tens' column.

You regroup whenever the sum in the ones' column is 10 or more. Sometimes you do not need to regroup.

Here is another example.

Add the ones. Regroup, if necessary.

Find the sum.	Regroup because $3 + 7 = 10$.	Add the tens.

```
 tens ones        tens ones           tens ones
                   1                   1
  3    3           3    3              3    3
+      7         +      7            +      7
────────        ─────────           ─────────
                        0              4    0
```

The answer is 40 or 4 tens and 0 ones.

Notice that when the sum in the ones' column is 10, you write 0 ones in the sum. That is because, when you regroup 10 ones as 1 ten, there are 0 ones left over.

Checking Addition by Changing the Order of the Addends

Remember that it does not matter what order you add numbers in, the sum is still the same. $7+3=10$ and $3+7=10$. You can check an addition problem by writing the addends in a different order, and then adding again. The sum should be the same both times.

You can check   by adding
addend   37 ———————————→ 55
addend   +55 ———————————→ +37

Let's do it:

add and regroup if necessary	add and regroup if necessary
tens ones	tens ones
1	1
3 7	5 5
+5 5	+3 7
9 2	9 2 ✓

You can check every two-digit addition problem in this way.

Adding Three Numbers

When you add three numbers, first add down.

To find the sum of	Add the ones. Regroup if necessary	Then add the tens. Regroup if necessary
tens ones	tens ones	tens ones
	1	1
4 3	4 3 ↓ add	add ↓ 4 3
2 8	2 8 ↓ down	down ↓ 2 8
+ 1 4	+ 1 4	+ 1 4
	5	8 5

When you are finished, add up to check your work.

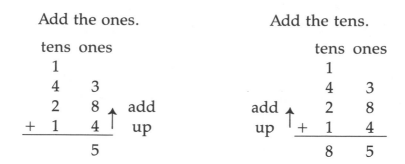

Add the ones.

```
tens ones
  1
  4    3
  2    8  ↑ add
+ 1    4  |  up
       5
```

Add the tens.

```
     tens ones
       1
       4    3
add ↑  2    8
up  | + 1   4
     8    5
```

You should get the same sum when you add up and when you add down.

Two-Digit Subtraction

Remember that to subtract from a two-digit number, first you subtract the ones. Then you subtract the tens.

Here's the problem.

```
tens ones
  9    7
- 5    5
```

Subtract the ones.

```
tens ones
  9    7
- 5    5
       2
```

Subtract the tens.

```
tens ones
  9    7
- 5    5
  4    2
```

The difference is 42.

Another Kind of Regrouping

Another way to regroup is to change 1 ten to 10 ones. Sometimes when you subtract, you need to do this kind of regrouping. Here is an example.
You have 27 pencils. You want to take away 9 pencils. But you only have 7 ones. You need to make one of the tens into 10 ones.

2 tens and 7 ones = 1 ten and 17 ones

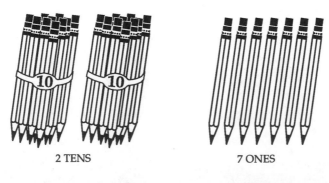

2 TENS   7 ONES

1 TEN

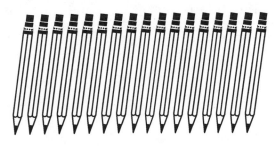

17 ONES

You have made 2 tens and 7 ones into 1 ten and 17 ones. Now you can take away 9 pencils easily.

 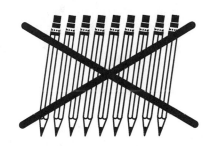 

There are 18 pencils left. $27 - 9 = 18$.

Practice this kind of regrouping. For example, write 58 as 4 tens and 18 ones. Write 8 tens and 13 ones as 93.

Subtracting Two-Digit Numbers with Regrouping

Sometimes you have to use this kind of regrouping when you are subtracting from a two-digit number. Look at the ones' column. If the number that you are taking away is greater than the number above it, you have to regroup.

Find the difference.   Regroup.

tens	ones		tens	ones
			5	**15**
6	5		6̶	5̶
− 4	8		− 4	8

8 is greater than 5. You can't take 8 away from 5. So you have to regroup. Change 65 to 5 tens and 15 ones. Cross out the 5 in the ones' place, and write 15 above it. Cross out the 6 in the tens' place, and write 5 above it. Now you can subtract easily. Remember to subtract the ones first.

Subtract the ones.   Subtract the tens.

tens	ones		tens	ones
5	**15**		**5**	**15**
6̶	5̶		6̶	5̶
− 4	8		− 4	8
	7		1	7

The difference is 1 ten and 7 ones, or 17.

Here is another example. Regroup, if necessary.

Find the difference.		Regroup.		Subtract the ones.		Subtract the tens.	
tens	ones	tens	ones	tens	ones	tens	ones
		7	**13**	**7**	**13**	**7**	**13**
8	3	8̶	3̶	8̶	3̶	8̶	3̶
−	8	−	8	−	8	−	8
					5	7	5

The difference of 83 and 8 is 75. Do not forget the 7 tens in your answer!

Checking Two-Digit Subtraction

Remember that you can check subtraction by addition.

To check   add like this:

```
  tens  ones          tens ones          tens ones           tens ones
                        5    12                                  1
    6     2             6     2             2     7             2     7
  − 3     5           − 3     5           + 3     5           + 3     5
  _____             _____             _____             _____
    2     7             2     7             6     2             6     2  √
```

The sum of the addition should be the same as the number you first subtracted from. 62 is the same as 62, which checks. Remember that addition is the opposite of subtraction.

Practice checking all two-digit addition and subtraction problems. You should do many two-digit addition and subtraction problems, until you can do them easily. If a problem does not check, begin it again. Try to find your mistake.

Adding and Subtracting Horizontally and Vertically

Adding or subtracting across is called adding or subtracting horizontally.

$$11 + 7 = 18$$
adding horizontally

$$23 - 12 = 11$$
subtracting horizontally

Adding or subtracting up or down is called adding or subtracting vertically.

```
  tens  ones                    tens  ones
    1     1                        2     3
  +       7                      − 1     2
  _____                        _____
    1     8                        1     1
```
adding vertically   subtracting vertically

Writing Addition and Subtraction Vertically

One way to add two-digit numbers that are written horizontally is to write them over again vertically.

Write 12 + 39 like this:

```
 tens  ones
   1    2
 + 3    9
 _____
```

Add the ones.

```
 tens  ones
   1
   1    2
 + 3    9
 _____
        1
```

Add the tens.

```
 tens  ones
   1
   1    2
 + 3    9
 _____
   5    1
```

The sum is 51.

Make sure that when you rewrite a problem vertically, you keep all the ones in the ones' column, and all the tens in the tens' column.

You can also rewrite subtraction vertically.

Write 23 − 12 like this:

```
 tens  ones
   2    3
 − 1    2
 _____
```

Subtract the ones.

```
 tens  ones
   2    3
 − 1    2
 _____
        1
```

Subtract the tens.

```
 tens  ones
   2    3
 − 1    2
 _____
   1    1
```

The difference is 11.

Adding or Subtracting Horizontally

Here is one way to add two-digit numbers horizontally. Find the sum of 57 + 32. Break the numbers down into tens and ones. Then add the tens and ones separately. 57 is the same as 50 + 7. 32 is the same as 30 + 2. 50 + 30 is 80 and 7 + 2 is 9. So the sum is 80 + 9 or 89.

The same method can be used to subtract two-digit numbers horizontally. Find the difference of 65 − 43. 65 is the same as 60 + 5 and 43 is the same 40 + 3. 60 − 40 = 20 and 5 − 3 = 2. So the difference is 22.

It is not easy to add or subtract this way when you need to regroup. Then it is better to write the problem vertically, if you have paper and pencil. Sometimes, though, you have to solve problems in your head without paper and

pencil. Then this is still a good method to use because it is easier to do in your head than trying to imagine subtracting vertically.

Another way to add or subtract in your head is to think of a fact you already know.

For example, $8+6=14$ In the same way, $15-8=\ 7$

so $18+6=24$ so $35-8=27$

and $48+6=54$ and $65-8=57$

Practice addition and subtraction problems like these a lot. Learn to solve a problem like $55+7=62$ in your head quickly.

Time

Telling Time to 5 Minutes

Remember that there are 60 minutes in 1 hour. 60 minutes is the amount of time it takes for the minute hand to go all the way around the clock. It is also the amount of time it takes for the hour hand to move from one number to the next number.

4 O'CLOCK

5 O'CLOCK

When the minute hand moves from one number to the next, 5 minutes have passed. For example, now it is 5 minutes after 4.

When the minute hand moves to the 2, it will be 10 minutes after 4. Count by fives for each new number to find how many minutes it has been since the hour. For example, when the minute hand is on the 7, it is 5, 10, 15, 20, 25, 30, 35 minutes after the hour.

The hour hand is between the 5 and the 6. That means it is after 5 o'clock, but it is not yet 6 o'clock. It is 35 minutes after 5.

Another way of writing 35 minutes after 5 is 5:35. The two dots : are called a colon. The number to the left of the colon tells the hours. The number to the right of the colon tells the minutes. 3:15 means 15 minutes after 3.

ON THIS CLOCK, IT IS 30 MINUTES AFTER 2, OR 2:30.

Remember that 30 minutes is half an hour. So 2:30 is also called "half past 2."

Practice counting around the clock face by fives. After practicing, you should be able to tell how many minutes each number shows without having to count. For example, when the minute hand is on the 8, you should know without counting that it is 40 minutes after the hour.

IT IS 5:40.

Sometimes when it is more than 30 minutes after the hour, we count backward around the clock to say how many minutes it is before the next hour. Here is an example.

It is 20 minutes before 6. 20 minutes before 6 is the same as 40 minutes after 5. This makes sense because 20 + 40 = 60, and there are 60 minutes in an hour. 20 minutes before 6 is also called 20 minutes to 6, or 20 minutes of 6.

How Much Time Has Passed

From 2 o'clock to 5 o'clock is 3 hours. Remember that the difference of 5 and 2 is 3. From 2:45 to 5:45 is also 3 hours. When the minutes are the same, the change in hours tells you how much time has gone by.

3 HOURS LATER

After 12 o'clock the next hour is 1 o'clock. From 10 o'clock to 1 o'clock is 3 hours, because it is 2 hours from 10 o'clock to 12 o'clock, and then one more hour to 1 o'clock.

A.M. and P.M.

Remember that A.M. refers to time before noon. The A.M. hours are between 12 midnight and 12 noon. Remember that P.M. refers to time after noon. The P.M. hours are between 12 noon and 12 midnight.

There are 12 A.M. hours and 12 P.M. hours in each day. Altogether there are 24 hours in a day.

The Calendar and Ordinal Numbers

Remember that ordinal numbers tell what number something is in an order. For example, January is the first month of the year, and June is the sixth month of the year. Last year, you learned the first twelve ordinal numbers.

We use ordinal numbers to say what day of the month it is. Most months have 31 days. In first grade you learned a rhyme which told you how many days each month has. Learn to say the ordinal numbers from thirteenth to thirty-first in order:

thirteenth	twentieth	twenty-seventh
fourteenth	twenty-first	twenty-eighth
fifteenth	twenty-second	twenty-ninth
sixteenth	twenty-third	thirtieth
seventeenth	twenty-fourth	thirty-first
eighteenth	twenty-fifth	
nineteenth	twenty-sixth	

Now learn to read the day of the month from a calendar.

OCTOBER

SUNDAY	MONDAY	TUESDAY	WEDNESDAY	THURSDAY	FRIDAY	SATURDAY
		1	2	3	4	5
6	7	8	9	10	11	12
13	14	15	16	17	18	19
20	21	22	23	24	25	26
27	28	29	30	31		

For example, the day colored in blue is Tuesday, October fifteenth. You know it is a Tuesday, because it is in the column under Tuesday. The day circled in black is Friday, October twenty-fifth.

Arabic and Roman Numerals

A numeral is a symbol used to show a number. For example, we use the numeral 7 to show the number seven. We also use the numeral 12 to show the number twelve. Languages other than English have different words for numbers like seven and twelve. There are also other kinds of numerals.

The numerals we usually use came from Arabia, and are called Arabic numerals. A different system came from ancient Rome. They are called Roman numerals. Here are some of the Roman numerals: one is I, two is II, five is V, ten is X.

Sometimes a clock face uses Roman numerals, instead of Arabic numerals. Learn how to write the Roman numerals from one to twelve from this clock face.

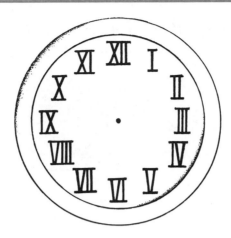

Notice that the Roman numeral I to the left of another Roman numeral means one less. V is five and IV is four.

Measurement

Measuring Length

Measuring how long something is is called measuring length. Length can be measured in different units. An inch is one unit for measuring length. The paper clip is 1 inch long. The leaf is 3 inches long.

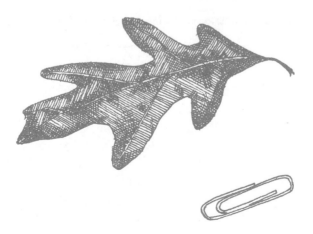

Learn to measure the length of different objects using a ruler marked in inches. You can also use a tape measure. A tape measure looks like this:

Most objects are not exactly a certain number of inches long. For example, the pencil is about 5 inches long.

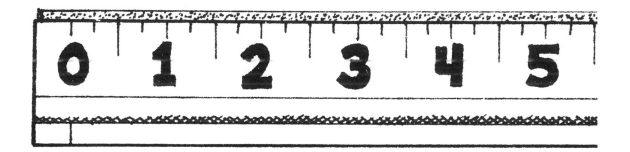

Learn to measure to the nearest inch.

Using a ruler, practice drawing line segments that are a certain number of inches long. For example, draw a line segment that is 7 inches long. You can read more about lines later in this chapter.

Also try this exercise. Draw a line segment 15 inches long. Put a mark after the first 8 inches. How long would you expect the rest of the line segment to be? Measure it, and see if you are correct.

Another unit for measuring length is a foot. A foot is 12 inches long. The plural of foot is feet. Learn to measure in feet and inches. Inches and feet are often abbreviated like this: in. and ft. An abbreviation is a short form of a word.

Measuring Weight

Measuring how heavy something is is called measuring weight. Measuring weight is also called weighing. One common unit for measuring weight is a pound. For example, the book weighs 1 pound.

A BOOK　　　　　**1 POUND WEIGHT**

When the balance is level, both sides weigh the same.

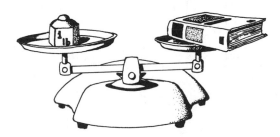

When a side of the balance is down, that side weighs more. The balance tells you that the pumpkin weighs more than a pound and that the apples weigh less than a pound. You should be able to list the objects from the lightest to heaviest like this: the apples, the book, the pumpkin.

The abbreviation for pounds is lb.

Numbers to 1,000

The Hundreds

10 tens is the same as 100. 100 is written out one hundred.

10 TENS

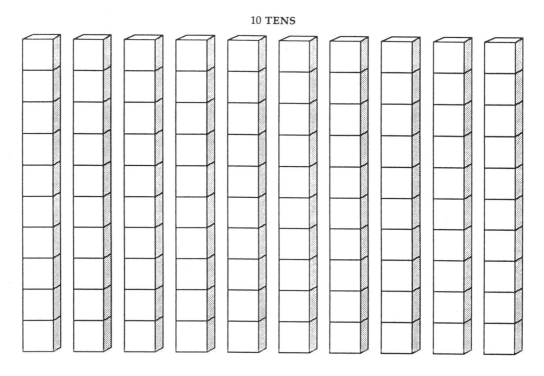

100

ONE HUNDRED

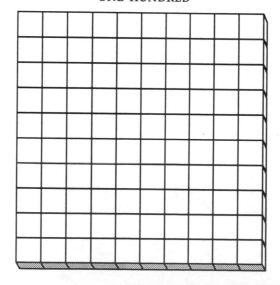

Notice that the number 100 has three digits.

three digits		hundreds	tens	ones
1 0 0		1	0	0

The first digit is the hundreds' place, the next digit is the tens' place, and the last digit is the ones' place.

The number with 2 hundreds is 200. 200 is written out two hundred.

200

TWO HUNDREDS

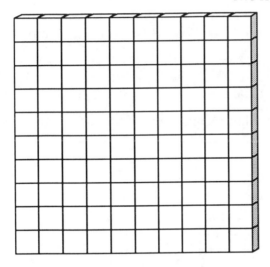 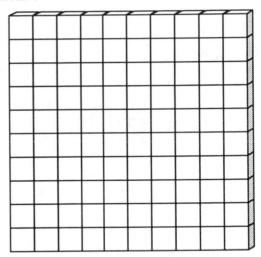

The number with 3 hundreds is 300.

These are the hundreds: 100, 200, 300, 400, 500, 600, 700, 800, 900. They are written out in words, like this: one hundred, two hundred, three hundred, four hundred, five hundred, six hundred, seven hundred, eight hundred, nine hundred. Learn to write the hundreds in numbers and in words.

Counting Between Hundreds

After 100, the numbers continue:

101, 102, 103, 104, 105, 106, 107, 108, 109, 110, 111, 112.

We say these numbers: one hundred one, one hundred two, one hundred three, one hundred four, one hundred five, one hundred six, one hundred seven, one hundred eight, one hundred nine, one hundred ten, one hundred eleven, one hundred twelve. We continue to count like this, beginning with one hundred each time, through all the numbers you already know, up to one hundred ninety-nine. After 199, the next number is a new hundred: 199, 200. As an example, here are the numbers from 185 to 200:

185, 186, 187, 188, 189, 190, 191, 192, 193, 194, 195, 196, 197, 198, 199, 200.

After 200, the numbers continue in the same way: 201, 202, 203, and so on, until we get to 299. After 299, the next number is 300. You count in this way all the way up to 999—nine hundred ninety-nine. After 999, the next number is 1,000. 1,000 is written out one thousand.

Practice counting from 100 to the next hundred. For example, practice counting from 300 to 400, or from 700 to 800. You should be able to count easily from one hundred to the next hundred.

Place Value

Remember that in a three-digit number each digit means something different. A 4 in the hundreds' place means 4 hundreds.

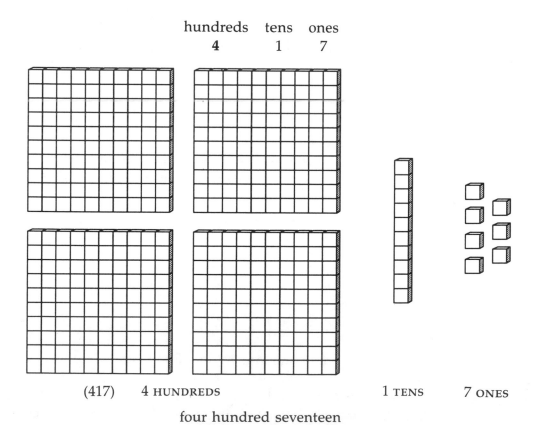

hundreds	tens	ones
4	**1**	**7**

(417)   4 HUNDREDS   1 TENS   7 ONES

four hundred seventeen

A 4 in the tens' place means 4 tens.

hundreds	tens	ones
2	**4**	5

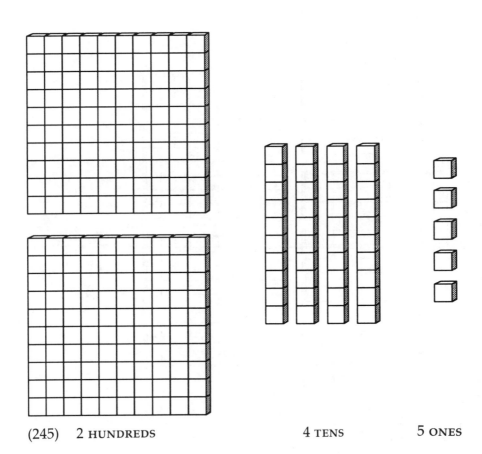

(245)   2 HUNDREDS   4 TENS   5 ONES

two hundred forty-five

A 4 in the ones' place means 4 ones.

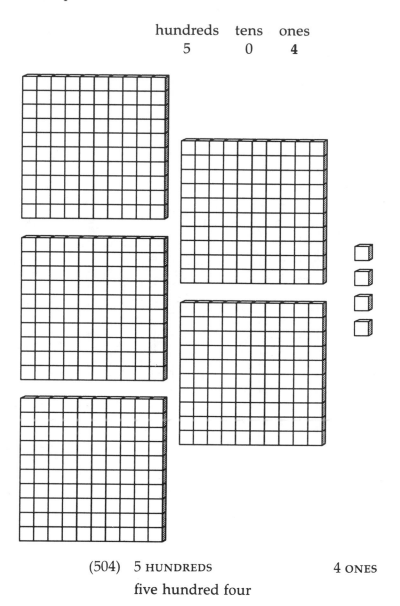

hundreds	tens	ones
5	0	**4**

(504)   5 HUNDREDS   4 ONES

five hundred four

The value of the different digits is called place value. Learn to show place value in different ways.

Practice writing a three-digit number in a place-value chart. For example, 673 is

hundreds	tens	ones
6	7	3

—place-value chart

Practice writing a three-digit number as hundreds, tens, and ones. For example, 514 is 5 hundreds, 1 ten, and 4 ones. You can see this easily from a place-value chart:

hundreds	tens	ones
5	1	4

Learn to write a three-digit number in expanded form. The expanded form of 273 is $200 + 70 + 3$. You already know that 73 is the same as $70 + 3$. Now you are learning that 273 is the same as $200 + 70 + 3$.

Remember that sometimes there are no tens or ones in a three-digit number. The expanded form of 603 is $600 + 3$. 340 is 3 hundreds, 4 tens, and 0 ones.

Comparing Three-Digit Numbers

Remember that numbers that come before in counting are less. 703 comes before 704, and 219 comes before 220. $703 < 704$ and $219 < 220$.

Remember that numbers that come after in counting are greater. 769 comes after 768 and 800 comes after 799. $769 > 768$ and $800 > 799$.

When comparing three-digit numbers to see which one is greater, always look at the hundreds' place first. If the hundreds' place is greater, then the number must be greater. For example, $611 > 596$. If the hundreds' place is the same, look at the tens' place to see which number is greater. For example, $371 > 359$. Only look at the ones' place if both the hundreds' place and the tens' place are the same. For example, $863 < 867$.

Writing Three-Digit Numbers

Learn to write three-digit numbers in words. For example, 843 is eight hundred forty-three. 707 is seven hundred seven. You already know how to write out the hundreds and the numbers up to one hundred. To write out three-digit numbers you only need to put these number words together.

Skip-Counting

Learn to count by hundreds to 1,000: 100, 200, 300, 400, 500, 600, 700, 800, 900, 1,000.

Learn to count by fifties to 1,000: 50, 100, 150, 200, 250, 300, 350, 400, 450, 500, and so on. Counting by fifties looks a little like counting by fives.

You should also learn how to count by tens with three-digit numbers. Here is an example of counting by tens, beginning with 110: 110, 120, 130, 140, 150. Sometimes when you count by tens you have to count through a hundred. For example, to complete the pattern 360, 370, 380, ___, ___, ___, ___, ___, you would count 390, 400, 410, 420, 430.

Learn to count by fives with three-digit numbers. Here is an example of counting by fives beginning with 575: 575, 580, 585, 590, 595, 600, 605, 610, 615.

Also learn to count by even numbers and odd numbers. Here is an example with even numbers: 736, 738, 740, 742, 744, 746, 748, 750. Here is an example with odd numbers: 489, 491, 493, 495, 497, 499, 501, 503, 505.

Sums and Differences of Three-Digit Numbers

ADDING THREE-DIGIT NUMBERS

To find the sum of three-digit numbers, first add the ones. Then add the tens. Then add the hundreds. Sometimes you have to regroup ones as tens. In a place-value chart, hundreds, tens, and ones are sometimes abbreviated as h, t, and o.

Find the sum.	Add the ones. Regroup, if necessary.	Add the tens.	Add the hundreds.
h t o	h t o	h t o	h t o
	1	**1**	1
2 5 3	2 5 **3**	2 5 3	2 5 3
+ 3 3 8	+ 3 3 **8**	+ 3 3 8	+ 3 3 8
	1	9 1	5 9 1

The sum is 591. When you are done, you should check your work by changing the order of the addends like this:

```
         h t o
           1
         3 3 8
       + 2 5 3
         5 9 1 √
```

REGROUPING TENS AS HUNDREDS

Sometimes when you add, you need to regroup tens as hundreds.

$$8 \text{ tens } + 4 \text{ tens } = 12 \text{ tens}$$

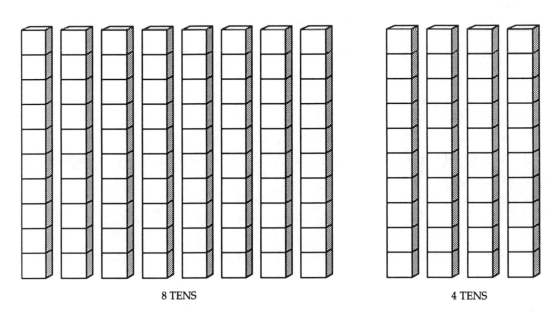

8 TENS   4 TENS

8 tens + 4 tens is 12 tens. Another way of showing 12 tens is to group 10 of the tens together to make 1 hundred.

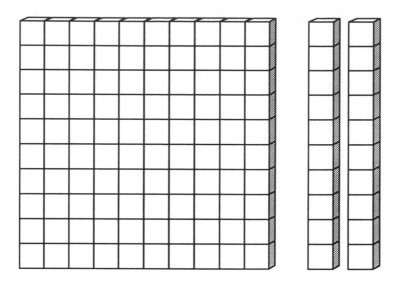

1 HUNDRED   AND   2 TENS

You have 2 tens left over. So 12 tens is the same as 1 hundred and 2 tens.

Practice regrouping in this way. For example, 7 tens + 8 tens = 15 tens. 15 tens = 1 hundred and 5 tens.

MORE ADDITION

In an addition problem when you have 10 or more tens, you regroup tens as hundreds.

Here is an example.

Find the sum.	Add the ones.	Add the tens. Regroup, if necessary.	Add the hundreds.
h t o	h t o	h t o 1	h t o 1
2 7 6	2 7 6	2 7 6	2 7 6
+ 6 6 3	+ 6 6 3	+ 6 6 3	+ 6 6 3
	9	3 9	9 3 9

The sum is 939.

In the tens' column, 7 tens + 6 tens makes 13 tens. 13 tens is the same as 1 hundred and 3 tens. So you write 3 at the bottom of the tens' column. Then you write 1 at the top of the hundreds' column for the new hundred. Then you add the hundreds.

Here is another example.

```
    h  t  o              h  t  o
       8  4                 8  4     15 tens =
   +   7  2             +   7  2     1 hundred and 5 tens
                          1  5  6
```

Add the ones
Add the tens   The sum is 156.
Regroup, if necessary

Notice in this problem how, after you regroup, you write the new hundred in the sum. Since there are no other hundreds, you do not need to carry the new hundred to the top of the hundreds' column.

MORE REGROUPING

Here is an example where you have to regroup both ones and tens.

Find the sum.	Add the ones. Regroup.	Add the tens. Regroup	Add the hundreds.
h t o	h t o	h t o	h t o
	1	**1 1**	**1 1**
6 3 8	6 3 8	6 3 8	6 3 8
+ 2 6 5	+ 2 6 5	+ 2 6 5	+ 2 6 5
	3	**0 3**	**9 0 3**

You should do many three-digit addition problems, until you can do them easily. Remember to check each addition problem by changing the order of the addends, and then adding.

SUBTRACTING FROM A THREE-DIGIT NUMBER

To subtract from a three-digit number, first subtract the ones. Then subtract the tens. Then subtract the hundreds. Remember that when the bottom number in the ones' column is greater than the top number in the ones' column, you need to regroup.

Begin with	Subtract the ones.	Subtract the tens.	Subtract the hundreds.
h t o	h t o	h t o	h t o
	7 12	7 12	7 12
5 8 2	5 8 2	5 8 2	5 8 2
− 2 6 9	− 2 6 9	− 2 6 9	− 2 6 9
	3	1 3	3 1 3

The difference is 313. Always check subtraction problems by addition like this:

h t o	h t o	h t o
7 12		1
5 8 2	3 1 3	3 1 3
− 2 6 9	+ 2 6 9	+ 2 6 9
3 1 3		5 8 2 √

MORE REGROUPING

There are 230 pencils. They are bundled together in 2 hundreds and 3 tens.

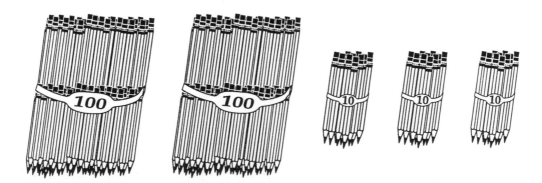

You want to take away 60 pencils. You can't do it, because there are only 3 tens. But if you make one of the hundreds into 10 tens, then you can take away 60 easily.

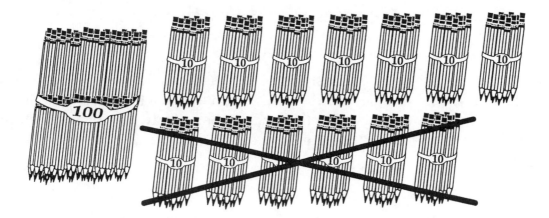

You regroup 2 hundreds and 3 tens as 1 hundred and 13 tens. Take 6 tens away. There are 1 hundred and 7 tens or 170 pencils left. So 230 − 60 = 170.

Practice regrouping in this way. For example, 3 hundreds and 4 tens is the same as 2 hundreds and 14 tens.

SUBTRACTION WITH REGROUPING 1 HUNDRED AS 10 TENS

Sometimes when you subtract you need to regroup 1 hundred as 10 tens. For example, to solve 556–372, you need to regroup because there are not enough tens.

Find the difference.	Subtract the ones.	Subtract the tens.	Subtract the hundreds.
h t o	h t o	h t o	h t o
		4 **15**	4 **15**
5 5 6	5 5 **6**	**5̶ 5̶** 6	**5̶ 5̶** 6
− 3 7 2	− 3 7 **2**	− 3 7 2	− 3 7 2
	4	8 4	1 8 4

The difference is 184.

You should do many three-digit subtraction problems, until you can do them easily. Remember to check each subtraction problem by addition.

Geometry and Fractions

Plane Shapes

Flat shapes are also called plane shapes. You already know these plane shapes: circles, triangles, rectangles, and squares. Learn to make triangles, rectangles, and squares in three ways. Practice tracing them, drawing them on graph paper with a ruler, and cutting them out of paper with a pair of scissors.

Figure

Another word for shape is figure. People often call plane shapes "plane figures."

Sometimes figure is used in a different way to mean a digit, or a number. If you are good at adding and subtracting, someone might say that you are "good at your figures." A three-digit number is called a "three-figure number."

Same Size, Same Shape

Learn to tell when shapes have the same shape and the same size. These two circles have the same shape, but not the same size.

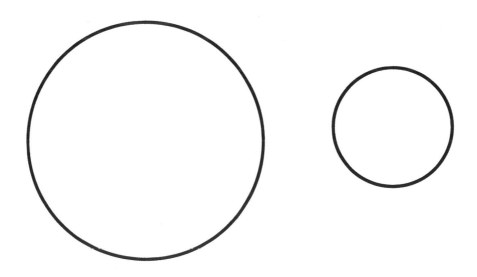

These two squares have the same shape and the same size.

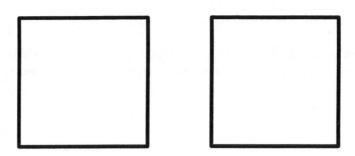

Points and Lines

A point is an exact spot. We show a point with a dot like this:　•　This point is called point A. Like this:　•
　　　　　　　　　　　　　　　　　　　　　　　　　A

A line is straight and goes on forever.

A LINE

The arrows show that the line continues forever in both directions. The line goes through points A and B, so it is called line AB or line BA. A short way to write line AB is $\overleftrightarrow{AB}$.

A　　　　　　　　　　　　B

A line segment is part of a line. A line segment is straight and has two endpoints.

A LINE SEGMENT

C   D

A line segment is named by its endpoints. This line segment is called line segment CD or line segment DC. A short way to write line segment DC is $\overline{DC}$.

Lines of Symmetry

When two shapes have the same shape and size, they match. A line that divides a shape into two parts that match is called a line of symmetry.

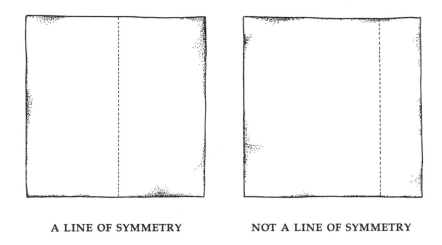

A LINE OF SYMMETRY   NOT A LINE OF SYMMETRY

Learn to fold paper shapes along a line of symmetry, so that the two parts match.

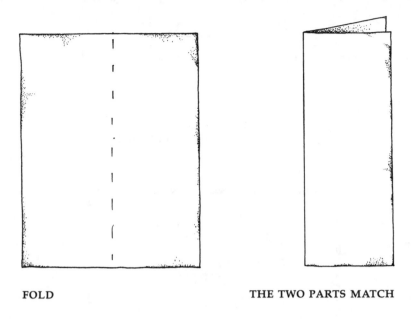

FOLD   THE TWO PARTS MATCH

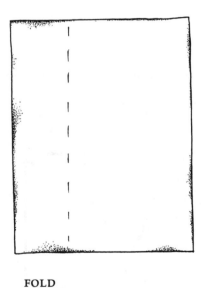
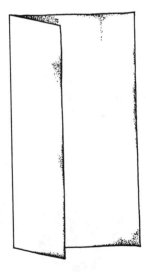

FOLD   THE TWO PARTS DO NOT MATCH

Some shapes do not have a line of symmetry. You cannot fold them so that the two parts match.

Interior and Exterior

The inside of a shape is called the interior, and the outside of a shape is called the exterior.

Exterior

Interior

Solid Shapes

You already know two solid shapes: spheres and cubes. Learn two more solid shapes, a cone and a cylinder.

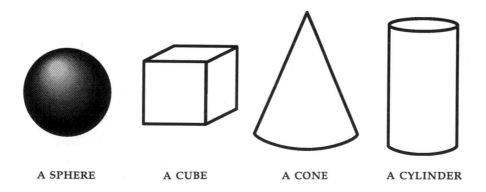

A SPHERE   A CUBE   A CONE   A CYLINDER

A cone looks like the cone of an ice cream cone. A cylinder looks like a can. Solid shapes are sometimes called solid figures.

Fractions

A fraction is a part of something. A fraction can be a part of one thing, like a circle, an apple, or a pizza. A fraction can also be a part of a group.

In first grade, you learned the fractions ½, ⅓, and ¼. They are written out one half, one third, and one fourth. Now you can learn the fractions ⅕, ⅙, and ¹⁄₁₀.

If something is divided into 5 equal parts, each part is ⅕. ⅕ is written out one fifth.

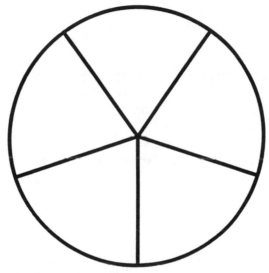

Each part is ⅕ of the circle.

If something is divided into 6 equal parts, each part is ⅙. ⅙ is written out one sixth.

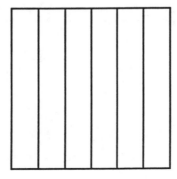

Each part is ⅙ of the square.

If something is divided into 10 equal parts, each part is ⅒. ⅒ is written out one tenth.

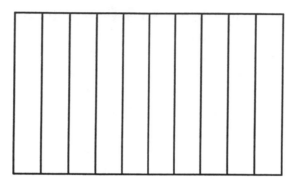

Each part is ⅒ of the rectangle.

Notice that each fraction has a top number and a bottom number. The bottom number tells how many equal parts there are. The top number tells how many of the equal parts you are talking about. Here are some examples.

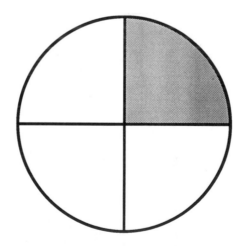

parts shaded: *1* is shaded
equal parts: 4
The circle has 4 equal parts. 1 of them is shaded. So ¼ of the circle is shaded.

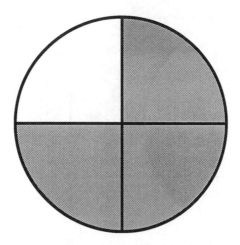

parts shaded: 3 are shaded
equal parts: 4
The circle has 4 equal parts. 3 of them are shaded. So ¾ of the circle is shaded. ¾ is written out three fourths.

Notice that ¼ is written out one fourth, and ¾ is written out three fourths. In the same way, ⅕ is written out one fifth, and ⅘ is written out four fifths.

Here are two more examples.

There are 10 equal parts.

3 of them are shaded. So 3/10 of the circle is shaded.

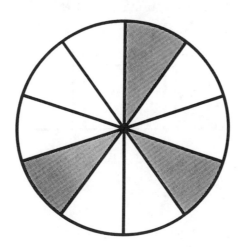

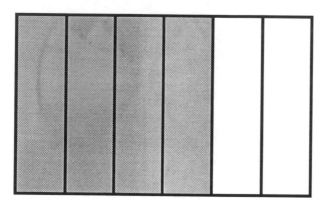

There are 6 equal parts.
4 of them are shaded.
So 4/6 of the rectangle is shaded.

Groups and Fractions

A fraction can also be a part of a group. When a fraction is part of a group, the bottom number tells how many there are in the group. The top number tells how many of the group you are talking about. Here is an example.

blue boxes 2
boxes 5

There are 5 boxes. 2 of them are blue. So ⅖ of the boxes are blue.

More Time

Remember that another word for one fourth is one quarter. 15 minutes is one quarter of an hour. That is why 4:15 is often called quarter past 4, or quarter after 4.

4:15   QUARTER PAST 4

Remember that 2:45 is also 15 minutes before 3. That is why 2:45 is also called quarter to 3.

2:45   QUARTER TO 3

Learn to tell time using "quarter" when the time is 15 minutes after an hour, or 15 minutes before an hour.

Money

Half Dollar and Dollar

You already know the value of the coins called penny, nickel, dime, and quarter. Learn the value of:

A half dollar. A half dollar is worth 50¢.

A 1-dollar bill. We write the amount 1 dollar
like this: $1.00 ("one dollar").
$1.00 is worth the same as 100¢.

Writing Amounts of Money

There are two ways of writing amounts of money: with the cents sign ¢, and with the dollar sign $.

When you write an amount of money with a dollar sign, the numbers to the right of the point are cents. For example, $1.47 is 1 dollar and 47 cents. $2.56 is 2 dollars and 56 cents.

Amounts less than a dollar are sometimes written with a dollar sign also.

$0.89 is the same as 89¢.

You read $0.89 and 89¢ in the same way: 89 cents.

Same Amounts

You already know different ways to make money add up to 25¢. Learn different ways to make up 1 dollar. Also learn some fractions of a dollar.

4 quarters make $1.00 A quarter is ¼ of a dollar.
2 half dollars make $1.00. A half dollar is ½ of a dollar.
10 dimes make $1.00. A dime is ¹⁄₁₀ of a dollar.
Also learn that 2 quarters make 50¢, and that 3 quarters make 75¢.

Counting Money

When you count money, count the dollars first. Then count the coins of largest value. Let's count the pictured money together.

Count the dollars. You have $3.00. A half dollar makes $3.50. 2 quarters are 50¢ more. That makes another dollar. You have $4.00. Count the coins that are left. 1 quarter makes $4.25. 3 dimes make $4.35, $4.45, $4.55. 3 nickels make $4.60, $4.65, $4.70. 4 pennies make $4.71, $4.72, $4.73, $4.74. Altogether $4.74 is pictured.

Practice counting money so that you can do it without making mistakes. Especially practice counting out a dollar with different coins. For example, a half dollar, a quarter, 2 dimes, and a nickel make $1.00.

Adding and Subtracting Money

You add and subtract amounts of money in the same way that you add and subtract other numbers. Here are some examples.

$$
\begin{array}{r}
1 \\
6\ 7\,\text{¢} \\
+\ 1\ 8\,\text{¢} \\
\hline
8\ 5\,\text{¢}
\end{array}
\qquad
\begin{array}{r}
1 \\
\$1.\ 8\ 5 \\
+\ \ 3.\ 6\ 4 \\
\hline
\$5.\ 4\ 9
\end{array}
\qquad
\begin{array}{r}
6\ \ 12 \\
\$6.\ 7\ \cancel{2} \\
-\ \ 4.\ 2\ 6 \\
\hline
\$2.\ 4\ 6
\end{array}
$$

Notice that you regroup in the same way when you add and subtract money. Do not forget to write the ¢ sign or the $ sign in your answer.

Word Problems

Learn to read a word problem, and decide what you must do to solve it. Then write the problem in numbers, and solve it.

A parking garage has 345 parking spaces underground and 275 parking spaces aboveground. How many parking spaces does the garage have in all?

This is an addition problem. You must add the parking spaces underground and the parking spaces aboveground to find how many parking spaces the garage has in all.

You write:	You add:	You check:
	1 1	1 1
3 4 5	3 4 5	2 7 5
+ 2 7 5	+ 2 7 5	+ 3 4 5
	6 2 0	6 2 0

The garage has 620 parking spaces.

   Margaret brings $3.65 to a movie. The movie ticket costs her $2.75. How much money does she have left?
   This is a subtraction problem. To figure out how much money Margaret has left, you must subtract the price of the ticket from the amount of money she brought.

You write:	You subtract:	You check:
	2 16	1
$3. 6 5	$3. 6 5	$0. 9 0
− 2. 7 5	− 2. 7 5	+ 2. 7 5
	$0. 9 0	$3. 6 5

Margaret has 90¢ left.

   Mr. Hale spends $6.47 on lunch. His friend, Mr. Hardy, spends $4.29. How much more does Mr. Hale spend than his friend?
   This is also a subtraction problem. If you take away the amount Mr. Hardy spends from the amount Mr. Hale spends, what you have left will be the extra amount Mr. Hale spends.

You write:	You subtract:	You check:
	3 17	1
$6. 4 7	$6. 4 7	$2. 1 8
− 4. 2 9	− 4. 2 9	+ 4. 2 9
	$2. 1 8	$6. 4 7

Mr. Hale spends $2.18 more than his friend.

   This kind of subtraction problem is very common. Whenever you want to find out how much more one amount is than another, you need to subtract.

Multiplication

Multiplication is a quick way of doing addition when you are adding the same number over and over again.

Here is an example.	$2+2+2+2+2=10$
You could also say:	5 twos $=10$
We write this as a multiplication problem:	$5 \times 2 = 10$
We read it:	Five times two equals ten.

The sign $\times$ means times. It shows that you are multiplying. Here is another example.

$$3+3+3+3=12$$
$$4 \text{ threes} = 12$$
$$4 \times 3 = 12$$

Multiplication Words

$$4 \times 3 = 12$$
factor factor product

Two numbers that are being multiplied are called factors. The answer is called the product. In $5 \times 2 = 10$, 5 and 2 are factors. 10 is the product.

Multiplication Tables

Multiplication is a very important part of arithmetic. In order to do multiplication, you need to learn the multiplication tables.

Learn the multiplication tables for 2, 3, 4, and 5. Next year you will learn the rest of the multiplication tables.

Two as a factor		Three as a factor		Four as a factor		Five as a factor	
$0 \times 2 = 0$	$5 \times 2 = 10$	$0 \times 3 = 0$	$5 \times 3 = 15$	$0 \times 4 = 0$	$5 \times 4 = 20$	$0 \times 5 = 0$	$5 \times 5 = 25$
$1 \times 2 = 2$	$6 \times 2 = 12$	$1 \times 3 = 3$	$6 \times 3 = 18$	$1 \times 4 = 4$	$6 \times 4 = 24$	$1 \times 5 = 5$	$6 \times 5 = 30$
$2 \times 2 = 4$	$7 \times 2 = 14$	$2 \times 3 = 6$	$7 \times 3 = 21$	$2 \times 4 = 8$	$7 \times 4 = 28$	$2 \times 5 = 10$	$7 \times 5 = 35$
$3 \times 2 = 6$	$8 \times 2 = 16$	$3 \times 3 = 9$	$8 \times 3 = 24$	$3 \times 4 = 12$	$8 \times 4 = 32$	$3 \times 5 = 15$	$8 \times 5 = 40$
$4 \times 2 = 8$	$9 \times 2 = 18$	$4 \times 3 = 12$	$9 \times 3 = 27$	$4 \times 4 = 16$	$9 \times 4 = 36$	$4 \times 5 = 20$	$9 \times 5 = 45$

Practicing Multiplication

Practice showing a multiplication problem with counters, like shells. Then you can count to find its product.

For example, to show 6×4, make 6 groups of 4, like this:

Count how many you have altogether. 24. So $6 \times 4 = 24$.

Also, learn to turn a multiplication problem into an addition problem. Then you can add to find the answer.

For example, 5×3 is the same as $3 + 3 + 3 + 3 + 3$.

$3 + 3 + 3 + 3 + 3 = 15$. So $5 \times 3 = 15$.

Notice that adding 3 over and over again is the same as counting by threes: 3, 6, 9, 12, 15. That is why when you count by threes, you get the products of the threes' table in order: $1 \times 3 = 3$, $2 \times 3 = 6$, $3 \times 3 = 9$, $4 \times 3 = 12$, $5 \times 3 = 15$.

Practice counting by twos, threes, fours, and fives. Count up to the last product in each multiplication table. This will help you learn the multiplication tables.

Make sure to practice showing multiplication as repeated addition. Here are two more examples.

4×2 is the same as $2 + 2 + 2 + 2$.

$5 + 5 + 5 + 5 + 5 + 5$ is the same as 6×5.

Multiplication Rules

Here are three important rules about multiplication.

1. It does not matter what order you multiply numbers in, the product is always the same.

$$5 \times 3 = 15 \quad \text{and} \quad 3 \times 5 = 15$$
$$7 \times 4 = 28 \quad \text{and} \quad 4 \times 7 = 28$$

2. When you multiply a number and one, the product is always that number.

$$1 \times 7 = 7 \qquad 5 \times 1 = 5$$

3. When you multiply a number and 0, the product is always 0.

$$0 \times 7 = 0 \qquad 5 \times 0 = 0$$

Learn these rules, and how to show multiplication problems with counters and by repeated addition. Then make sure you can find all the products in the multiplication tables for 2, 3, 4, and 5 quickly and easily. Practice saying the multiplication table for each number. Say the whole of each equation, like this: "Six times two equals twelve." "Seven times two equals fourteen."

If it is easier for you, you can put the factor that is the same each time first. Here is an example: $3 \times 0 = 0$, $3 \times 1 = 3$, $3 \times 2 = 6$, $3 \times 3 = 9$, and so on.

Word Problems

Learn to solve word problems using multiplication.

Lisa has 4 boxes. In each box she has 5 bottles of orange juice. How many bottles of orange juice does she have?

This is a multiplication problem because Lisa has the same number of orange juice bottles in each box. To solve it, you could add 5 bottles of orange juice over and over again, or you could multiply 4×5. You write: $4 \times 5 = 20$. Lisa has 20 bottles of orange juice.

V.

NATURAL SCIENCES

Introduction to Life Sciences

In this section, children are introduced to botany and zoology, and to the life cycle of birth, growth, reproduction, and death. The cycle of life is connected with the seasons, and the cycle of the seasons is explained. The help of the parent or teacher is much needed in explaining the seasons to young children.

Most adults know that the seasons are not determined by the earth's rotation, which simply causes the daily cycle of light and dark. But gaps in our educational system have left many parents and teachers with a rather unclear understanding of the cycle of the seasons. Polls show that many Americans think the earth is closer to the sun in summer than in winter. In fact, the earth is farthest away from the sun in our summer, and closest in winter, though the difference in distance is of minor importance. It is the tilt of the earth on its axis (toward the sun in summer and away from the sun in winter) as it journeys around the sun that causes the seasonal changes of winter and summer. To help children understand the seasons in North America, it will be most useful to use a physical model. Here's a simple suggestion for one.

The seasonal relationship between the earth and the sun can be illustrated to a child by putting a knitting needle through a tennis ball to simulate the earth and its axis. The equator should be drawn at right angles to the knitting needle. The tennis ball can then be circled around a burning light bulb in a plane parallel to the floor at the same height as the bulb, keeping the axis at a constant tilt toward the north. As the ball circles close to the bulb, the dark and light sides of the ball will be clearly seen, and so will the differences in light intensity on different parts of the ball.

The critical element in this demonstration is to keep the knitting needle tilted at a constant angle to the north as the ball goes around the light bulb. At one point in the ball's orbit around the light, the top part of the knitting needle will be pointed toward the axis of the bulb. At this point (high summer), the light will shine brightly on the top part of the ball. Half an orbit later, when the top part of the needle is pointed away from the axis of the bulb, light will fall dimly on the top of the ball. Point out to the child that just the opposite is happening to the bottom part of the ball.

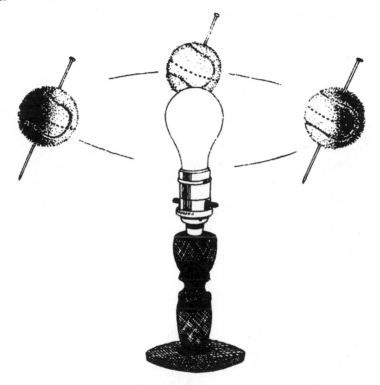

By holding the knitting needle at the same angle throughout the orbit around the light bulb, children can see that we have the seasons because the slant of our axis stays constant with respect to the sun. Probably, nothing short of an actual demonstration of this unchanging tilt can make the causes of the seasons clear.

A child's knowledge of the natural world must be gained chiefly by observation and experience, not mainly from books. To understand the plant and animal worlds, a child must observe plants and animals, preferably in natural settings, and, at second-best, in museums and school laboratories. But book-learning does have tremendous importance in bringing system and coherence to a young child's knowledge of nature. Only through systematic presentation of topics can a child make steady and secure progress in scientific learning. The child's development of scientific knowledge and understanding is in some ways a very disorderly and complex process, different for each child. But a systematic approach to the topics of life sciences can at least provide essential building blocks for deeper understanding at a later time. Such a systematic approach ensures that huge gaps in knowledge will not hinder later understanding.

Besides presenting an overview of the seasons and the cycle of life, this second book also explains cells, organs, and some elementary facts about health and nutrition. The rationale for our selections bears repeating. In making this selection of topics for beginning life sciences, our committees were guided both by their wide experience in teaching young children, as well as by the careful sequences that have been developed in nations that have had outstanding results in teaching elementary science: Sweden, West Germany, France, and Japan. In addition, our committee members consulted reports by the American Association for the Advancement of Science, and had discussions with the staff of the National Science Foundation. There is no one best sequence for the systematic development of knowledge about life sciences, but we are certain that the one chosen is a good one that has proved itself to be effective.

That said, I must repeat: no sequence can be truly effective without direct, hands-on experience of and observation of the natural world. Children also need imaginative help from parents and teachers in stimulating their natural interest in the natural world.

Life Sciences

What Are the Life Sciences?

There is a special science that studies all living things from houseflies to oak trees. It is called "biology." Biologists study how living things started—where they came from, and how they grow. They study how living things are put together, and how they behave. Biologists are constantly finding out more about living things.

You can be a biologist too! These two friends are investigating a pond.

There is a special part of biology that deals with plants. It's called "botany." Botanists ask questions like: Why does the sap of trees flow in the spring? How do plants purify the air? How do plants make more plants just like themselves? If you like to grow plants and study them, you may someday become a botanist, and answer questions like these.

Another part of biology studies animals. It's called zoology. Does "zoology" remind you of the zoo? Well, it should, because the word "zoo" is short for

Here's a way to remember the two parts of biology—a house with two doors.

"zoological garden," which means garden of the animals. Zoologists ask questions like: Where do frogs live in the winter? How do caterpillars become beautiful butterflies? Why do some birds fly south in the winter? You already know something about zoology if you have a pet that you have to keep healthy.

The Cycle of Life

All living things are born, grow, and eventually die. To keep their kind going after they die, they need to produce young like themselves—a process called reproduction. Here's an example of reproduction: A chicken lays an egg. Out of the egg hatches a chick. The chick grows up to be a hen. The hen mates with a rooster, who fertilizes her egg. The hen lays the egg. Out of the egg hatches a chick. The cycle starts again. Let's look at a picture of this cycle. Where is the beginning of the cycle, and where is the end? There is no beginning or end. There is an old question: "Which came first, the chicken or the egg?" Nobody has yet found an answer. Which do you think came first?

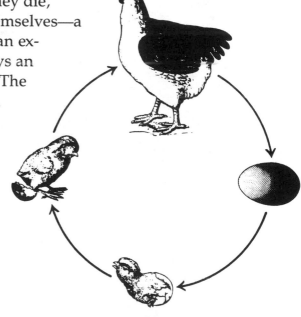

This picture can help you imagine the reproduction cycle of a chicken.

Reproduction

What is reproduction? You know that to produce something means to *make* something. A farmer produces vegetables. To reproduce something means to make something that is like itself. When you copy a page on a Xerox machine you *reproduce* the page. Animals have to reproduce themselves so life can keep going on. Chickens must have chicks for chickens to go on. Human parents must have children, so human beings will go on. Without reproduction, the cycle of life would stop.

Living things reproduce themselves in different ways, but very often it happens like this: In plants, male pollen from a flower fertilizes a female ovule of a flower. The fertilized ovule becomes a seed. If the seed is put in soil and watered, it will grow into a new baby plant.

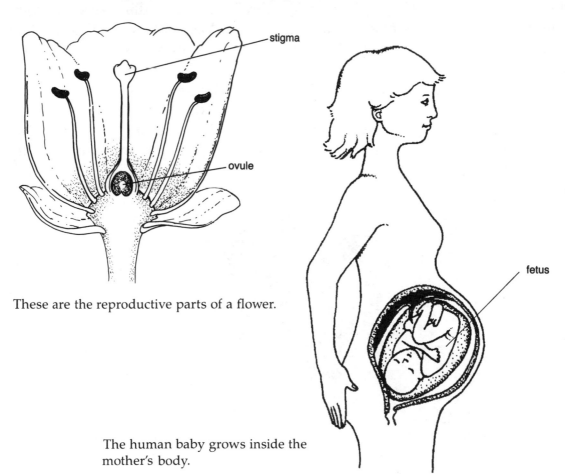

stigma

ovule

These are the reproductive parts of a flower.

fetus

The human baby grows inside the mother's body.

In animals, the process often works the same way, as we saw with chickens and eggs. A male sperm fertilizes a female ovum. The ovum becomes a fertilized egg. If the egg is given the right conditions to grow, it will develop into a new baby.

The Cycle of the Seasons

Now we know that the cycle of life has four parts: birth, growth, reproduction, and death. In some living things, the cycle of life follows the cycle of the four seasons of the year—spring, summer, fall, and winter. A sunflower seed sprouts from the ground in the springtime. The plant grows in the summer. The seeds from this adult plant ripen in the fall. Some of the ripe seeds fall on the ground. The plant dies in winter. The next spring a seedling sprouts from one of the fallen seeds and becomes a new sunflower plant. Just as the life cycle repeats itself, so the cycle of the four seasons happens over and over again, every year.

To find out why, you have to know that the earth goes around the sun. Last year we learned that the earth spins like a top, making a full spin once every day. The spin causes day and night because when the spinning earth faces the sun it's daytime, and when the spinning earth is turned away from the sun, it's nighttime.

It takes the earth one year to orbit around the sun.

But the spinning of the earth only makes day and night. It doesn't make spring, summer, fall, and winter. The four seasons are made by the earth slowly traveling around the sun in a big egg-shaped circle called an "orbit." It takes exactly one year for the earth to go completely around the sun and come back where it started from. The earth has taken this same trip every year since before life began, round and round in the same orbit. Whenever the earth reaches the same place on its trip, one year has passed.

Whenever the earth is in the same place on its trip, the calendar will say it's the same date. What day and month is it today? In exactly 365 days from now, which is one year from now, the earth will again be in the same place in its journey around the sun. As the earth goes on its 365-day round trip, the months pass and the weather changes. Have you noticed that in July and August the weather is warm, but in January and February the weather is cooler? Let's find out why.

> Can you say all the months of the year, from January to December? If you can, you can make a picture of where the earth will be in each month as it travels around the sun.

Why Is Summer Hot? Why Is Winter Cold?

Why do the different seasons have different temperatures? Why is it hot in summer and cold in winter? Why is the temperature in-between in spring and fall? It's because the earth doesn't stand straight up and down as it travels around the sun. Instead, the earth is tilted. When it is summer, our part of the earth is tilted toward the sun. That makes the sunlight shine strongly on us, and makes the weather hot. When it is winter, our part of the earth is tilted away from the sun, and the sunlight shines on us weakly. Have you noticed that the light gets less bright in the winter? That makes wintertime colder. It's colder because we are getting less heat from the sun.

In this picture North America is tilted toward the sun. Is it winter or summer in North America in this picture?

Depending on where you live in the United States, the temperature can change a lot from one season to another. If you live in the Northern states there is a lot of difference between summer and winter. That's because the Northern states are tilted toward the sun in summer, but tilted away from the sun in winter.

There is less difference in Southern states. Can you guess why? Do you remember reading about the equator? The area at the equator stays nearly the same warm temperature all year. Our Southern states are nearer the equator than the Northern ones so they get more warmth from the sun's rays all year long.

Now that you know why there are different temperatures in the different seasons, let's follow the four seasons for one year, to see how plants and animals adjust to the different temperatures. Let's start with the spring, when life begins again.

Spring

Spring is an exciting time of year! The temperature begins to get warmer. After the cold winter, the natural world seems to wake up and come alive. Maple trees begin to send sap, a sugary liquid, up to their branches so that new leaves will have food to start growing. Sunflower seeds that rested all winter send roots into the warm soil and sprout little seedlings of sunflower plants.

Animals that slept all winter wake up and come out of their nests and dens. Squirrels hurry about. Young bears born during the winter join their mothers in search of food.

Birds, butterflies, and whales return from their long trip south and begin to mate in order to reproduce. Birds build nests so they can lay their eggs and tend them until they hatch.

Frogs also mate in the spring and lay their eggs in water. The eggs hatch into tadpoles, which breathe through gills and swim in the water.

Insect eggs that lay quietly all winter now hatch. Out come tiny grasshoppers to feed on the new plant leaves!

Can you guess the name of one of the most beautiful creatures to come out in spring? It's an animal that changes itself from a wormlike caterpillar into a lovely creature that can fly! You're right! A butterfly!

The warmth of spring starts life over again, until spring gradually turns into summer.

This girl has discovered a bird's nest. Notice that she is not touching the nest.

The Stages of the Butterfly Cycle.

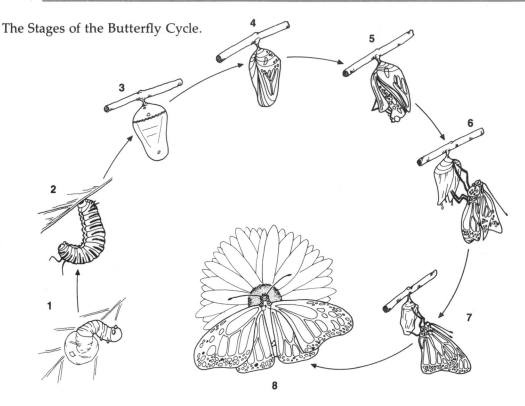

1. A caterpillar, or butterfly larva, hatches from its egg.

2. The caterpillar (larva) grows larger.

3. The fully grown caterpillar crawls onto a twig and covers itself in a special case called a cocoon. This is the pupa stage of the butterfly.

4. Inside the pupa, the butterfly begins to form.

5. The butterfly hatches from its case.

6. Weak, damp, and crumpled, the butterfly emerges.

7. The butterfly expands its wings. When the wings have dried, the butterfly is ready for flight.

8. The adult butterfly sits on a flower.

Summer

In the hot summer most plants and animals continue to grow. Temperatures are warm enough that even cold-blooded animals like snakes can move fast. Have you ever seen a snake or lizard lying in the early morning summer sun? These animals are easy to catch at this time because they move slowly. Later on in the day, when the sun warms them up, they can move fast.

Tadpoles grow into adult frogs in the early summer. Sunflower and corn seedlings grow into plants and begin to develop seeds. Young insects like grasshoppers grow into adults.

Bear cubs are growing. So are the baby birds that hatched out of their eggs in the spring. Summer is a time when young creatures begin to fend for themselves. Trees add many inches to their branches. Flowers begin to make seeds. Summer is a time of joy, activity, and growing.

Fall

Fall is a time of ripeness and fullness. Seeds ripen, apples turn red, and old age comes to plants that live just one year. Plants like corn and the sunflower have a life span of only one year. Each kernel of corn that develops in early fall is a fertilized seed. These seeds can fall to the earth. The corn plant dies. The seeds will lie asleep in the soil all winter.

Plants that live longer begin to prepare for the cold, hard times that are coming. You remember that deciduous plants lose their leaves in fall? They drop their leaves so they don't have to work hard making food in the winter. They go dormant, which means they go to sleep. Plants that go dormant in the fall will live through the winter from the food stored in their roots.

Squirrels begin scurrying back and forth, their cheeks stuffed with nuts.

What's their hurry? They know that winter is coming. They gather nuts to store for food during the cold months.

In the fall, bears look for winter dens to protect them from the winter weather. They stay close to these dens, eating as much as they can to build up the extra fat which they will live on during their long winter sleep.

What do birds do in the fall? Sometimes you can see great flocks of them flying overhead. They are going on a long flight south, where the winter weather will be warm.

Some birds fly as far as South America to feed in the warm sunshine there.

These Canadian geese fly south for the winter in the shape of a V.

Others, like robins, fly only as far south as the southern United States. And some birds, like cardinals, do not migrate at all. They spend all year in the same area, feeding on winter berries and whatever seeds they can find.

When it gets colder, marine animals such as whales migrate to warmer waters. Gray whales travel between three thousand and seven thousand miles. That means that sometimes they travel as far as you would if you crossed the United States twice!

Fall is a time of great preparation for many animals and plants. They are getting ready for the hardest time of the year.

Winter

In winter, life moves more slowly, or comes almost to a stop. Even tropical areas like Hawaii and parts of southern Florida look and feel different in winter. Some plants die back in response to less heat and sunlight: their stems

A red fox alone on the snow.

and leaves wither while their roots sleep under the ground. Many trees go to sleep while they live off food stored in their trunks and roots. Seeds lie asleep in the soil.

Animals conserve their energy. Tree squirrels spend most of their time in their nests, eating nuts and sleeping. Ground squirrels and chipmunks sleep in their holes all winter, living off fat they built up in summer and fall. This is called "hibernating." Their breathing and their heartbeat slow down, so they need much less food and water than when they are active.

Animals such as frogs and snakes hibernate also. Although they are called cold-blooded animals, their blood isn't really cold all the time. It's the same temperature as the air or water around them. As the weather gets cold, their blood temperature goes down, and they have to slow down. Frogs just burrow into the cold mud at the bottom of the pond and wait for better times.

Bears sleep through the winter in their dens, but some scientists say they are not true hibernators, because their body temperature and heartbeat do not change much. Female black bears actually give birth to their young in winter dens. The young grow big and strong by feeding on their mother's milk and emerge from the den with her in early spring.

Animals that migrated to the South in the fall spend their winters resting and feeding in South America or the warm Southern states. They must build up their strength for the long trip north in the spring!

The Human Body and Health

Cells

Do you remember reading about the major parts of your body last year? You read about your skin, your skeleton, your muscles, and your teeth. Each of these body parts is made up of different kinds of cells. Cells are the building blocks of all plants and animals, so they are the building blocks of your body. Have you ever heard of a jail cell? It's a small room that is closed up so a person can't get out. The little units of living things are also called cells, because they are like tiny closed rooms. Cells are

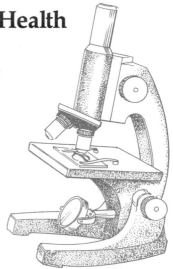

This is a microscope.

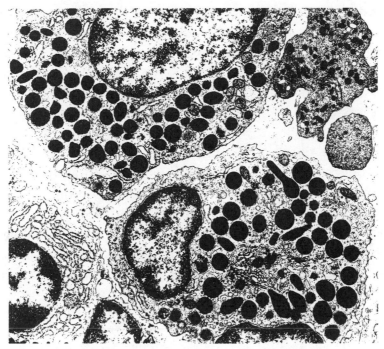

When you look through a microscope, you might see something like these cells.

so small you need a microscope to see them. The contents of the cell are surrounded by something like a very, very thin skin. All plants and animals are made up of these tiny cells.

Tissues and Organs

A lot of cells join together to make up tissues. Different tissues join together to form organs, like the heart, lungs, and stomach. Your lungs are made out of lung tissues. And your lung tissues are made of lung cells. Your brain is made out of brain tissues. And your brain tissues are made of brain cells. The kinds of cells that make your lung tissues are different from the kinds that make your brain tissues. In your body, there are many, many different kinds of cells, making up different kinds of tissues and organs.

Systems: Parts That Work Together

Some tissues and organs of the body work together like members of a team. The parts that work together are called a "system." Your nerves and the tissues around them work together as members of your nervous system. Your mouth, throat, stomach, and intestines work together as members of your digestive system. Your breathing muscles and your lungs work together to form your breathing system, which is also called your respiratory system. You have several other systems that we will talk about later. Right now we will talk about your digestive system.

Traveling Through the Digestive System

Do you remember reading about the five senses, and how they are used when you eat an apple? Well, your body uses these five senses—sight, hearing, touch, smell, and taste—every time you eat or drink something, to start the digestive process. Yes, even before you put food in your mouth, your digestive system is getting ready for it. Your brain has received all the sensory messages but taste, and it sends messages to your mouth and your stomach. The message is: *get ready, food is coming!*

When you pop that piece of apple in your mouth, your tongue tastes it,

It is important to eat three balanced meals a day.

and what happens? Your mouth "waters." Where does all that liquid come from? First, your tongue picks up the sweet taste of the apple and sends messages to your brain: "Here's something good." Your brain receives the "sweet" message from the apple, and tells the salivary glands in your mouth to let out more saliva. Saliva is a special liquid your mouth makes. It has water and chemicals called "enzymes" that help digest food. The salivary glands are where all the liquid comes from.

The piece of apple is still too big for you to swallow, so what do you do? Chew! The eight teeth in the front of your jaws, four on top and four on bottom, are called incisors. They bite the piece of apple into smaller pieces, and then your four pointy canine teeth next door tear it up. Your tongue helps to push it to the back of your mouth, where your bicuspids and molars are. Bicuspids have two bumps on them which help crush the piece of apple, and your flat molars grind it into tiny pieces you can swallow.

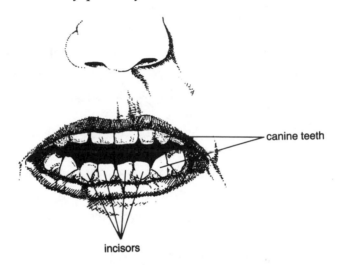

Now the pieces of apple are small enough for you to swallow so you gulp, and down they go. The apple goes down your throat, through your esophagus, and into your stomach. And your stomach is ready for it!

Your stomach is really a big muscle that grinds up the food you eat. It also sends out an acid to help change what you eat into nutrients your body can use. (You've heard of nutrition, haven't you? It means nourishing or feeding.) The stomach releases these nutrients into your small intestine. The small intestine then begins to absorb the food into the blood. The blood brings the nutrients to all the cells of your body.

What happens to the leftover materials in the small intestine, the things that can't be digested? This solid waste moves from your small to your large intestine. This is the last part of the journey. Water from the leftovers is absorbed into the blood. Finally, the solid waste passes out of your body through the anus as feces.

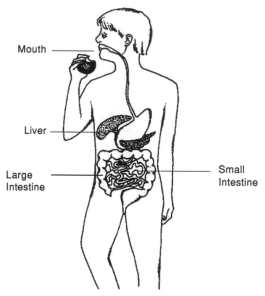

Mouth

Liver

Large
Intestine

Small
Intestine

The digestive system.

Your body makes urine in a totally separate process. This story starts with the blood, which carries waste away from the cells of the body. The blood goes through the kidneys, which separate out the urine from the blood. The urine is stored in the bladder until it passes out of your body through the urethra.

You notice we didn't say anything about your appendix. It is a little tube connected to your large intestine. You or somebody you know may have had an appendix taken out because sometimes it gets swollen and sore. But it's okay to take it out because it isn't necessary to have it.

What a long trip that piece of apple took! Let's trace the trip again. Mouth to esophagus; esophagus to stomach; stomach to small intestine, small intestine to large intestine; remaining solids pass out of the body. But water goes from the large intestine into the blood. And eventually the kidney extracts the liquid called urine from the blood and it passes out of the body, too.

The Right Foods: Doing Your Part

Now you know how your body gets nutrients from the foods you eat. It's very, very important to eat the right nutrients, so your body can grow properly. You need different kinds of foods from the four main food groups. They are: 1) meat or fish, 2) dairy products, 3) breads and cereals (whole-grain ones are best), and 4) fresh fruits and vegetables.

Meat and fish.

What kinds of nutrients do we mainly get from these foods? Meat and fish give us proteins, which help make new cells. Milk and cheese give us proteins and fats. Fats are stored in our body and provide long-lasting energy for

Dairy foods.

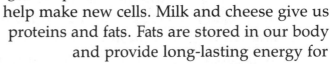
Breads and cereals.

our cells. Breads and cereals give us carbohydrates, which provide quick energy and fiber, which helps us digest our foods more efficiently. Fruits and vegetables give us both fiber and special doses of vitamins and minerals which help our bodies stay strong and healthy.

Fruits and vegetables.

Vitamins and Minerals

All these foods have chemicals called vitamins and minerals which need to be eaten in the right amounts to keep us healthy. Vitamin A from carrots and other vegetables gives us healthy skin, hair, tissues, and eyes. Vitamin C from oranges and other citrus fruits protects cells and helps growth. Vitamin D, found in milk, helps us have strong teeth and bones. Calcium and phosphorus are minerals necessary for building strong bones. Calcium also helps our muscles work. Other minerals help out, too. Potassium and sodium (found in table salt) help our nerves work well. And iron, found in many foods, helps the blood do its job. You'll get all these vitamins and minerals if you eat the right amounts of each food group.

A Balanced Diet

If you don't eat enough foods from these main food groups, you might suffer from poor nourishment, which is called "malnutrition." Now that you know about the nutrients your body needs, and what they help it do, you can easily understand how malnutrition can lead to a very unhealthy body. Too little nutritious food is unhealthy, but so is too much. It is important to eat a balanced diet—a moderate amount of food from each group.

The biologists who study nutrition now tell us it is important to cut down on fats found in foods like butter, ice cream, and french fries, and to eat more foods with fiber. Whole-grain breads and cereals have large amounts of fiber in them. And it helps to cut down on foods like soda pop and chocolate, which have large amounts of sugar in them.

You can practice healthy eating habits every day and enjoy a healthier body as a result!

Keep a record of each meal—breakfast, lunch, and dinner—you eat every day for a week. Then you can see if you manage to eat a well-balanced diet. If you aren't eating a well-balanced diet, you can make a list of the foods you need to eat more of and the foods you need to eat less of.

Introduction to Physical Sciences

FOR PARENTS AND TEACHERS

In Book II, the selection and ordering of subjects was decided in exactly the way that was described in the introduction to the life sciences. The topics in this book cover the activities and aims of the different physical sciences: chemistry, physics, astronomy, earth science, and meteorology. In addition, children are introduced to important subjects in technology. There is discussion of engineering. Explanations are given of simple tools like the wedge and inclined plane. Children are introduced to the importance of iron and steel, the characteristics of magnets, how to find directions out of doors, and what makes the colors of the rainbow.

Just as in life sciences, so here, the main teacher of the young child is experience. A famous experiment by the Swiss psychologist Piaget shows that very young children think a tall narrow glass holds more water than a squat thick one, when in fact the glasses hold the same amount. Later on, children do not make this mistake. How have children learned a truer understanding of the physical world? Not from books and science teachers, but from experience: by getting their hands wet and dirty with the size and heft of things, by noticing that when they toss a rock up it falls back down, by noticing that thunder comes after lightning.

Unfortunately, not all children come to school with equal amounts of experience and knowledge of the physical world. One of the main tasks of science teaching in the very early grades is to fill in the important gaps for all children. This must be done systematically in a planned sequence, even if it means going over ground already familiar to some children. But we have tried to make the familiar interesting, too. We hope there will be something new and interesting for every child.

As in the previous book, we have tried to encourage hands-on observation and experimentation.

Physical Sciences

What Is Chemistry?

Have you ever asked why a bee sting hurts, or what makes lemons taste sour? Have you wondered why nails rust, or why water rolls off a duck's feathers? These are the kinds of questions scientists try to answer in the science called chemistry. If you have thought about these things, you might decide to find out more about chemistry, the study of matter.

From the beginning of human life, people have always wanted to know what things are made of. Even in ancient times, before the Greeks, humans discovered that they could make hard bricks for building houses if they mixed together clay, water, and straw, and then dried the mixture in the sun. They noticed that water from the ocean tasted saltier than water from a stream. They learned that rocks would not burn. They noticed that different types of matter behaved differently.

The ancient Greeks tried to find out about matter step by step. They wrote down their ideas, and we can still read what they thought. They said that everything is made out of four basic kinds of matter: earth, air, fire, and water. Today, scientists know that isn't right, but people still respect the ideas of the Greeks, because they studied the natural world so carefully.

Later on, people called alchemists began to study matter for their own gain. They thought they could become rich by changing cheap metals like iron into expensive gold. They tried everything they could think of, but no gold ever appeared. Even though the alchemists did not succeed, their experiments taught them many new things about matter.

Today, chemists not only learn what past ages knew about matter, they also gain new knowledge. Now we know more about matter than ever before. But chemists still have plenty to learn. They are still finding out how different materials can be mixed together to make new things. Let's find out more about what chemists do today.

What Do Chemists Do?

Chemists check whether the air that we breathe is pure, and whether the food we eat is safe and healthful. They find out whether the water that comes out of lakes and rivers is clean, and if it isn't, they purify and retest it to make certain that it is safe for us to drink.

Chemists make strong, light plastics used for football helmets. They make fuels for jet planes. They make materials for clothes. Read the label inside the collar of your shirt or sweater. Do you see the words "acrylic" or "polyester"? These materials were developed by chemists so that we can wear inexpensive, comfortable, "wash-and-wear" clothes.

Chemists make medicines that help cure sickness. Years ago, people used to die from a sickness called malaria. But there were some South American Indians who knew how to get well from the disease. Whenever they got sick from malaria they chewed on the bark of a tree named the cinchona, and something in the bark made them get well. Chemists learned to remove the healing substance from the bark and called it quinine, from the word cinchona. After that, people in other parts of the world who were sick with malaria could get well by taking pure quinine as a medicine. Chemists today are still making new medicines that help keep our bodies healthy.

What Is Physics?

Those who study physics ask such questions as how do things move? And what makes them move? Physicists want to know how things act when they are pushed or pulled, or get bumped. They also study the forces that make things move, and measure how fast they go. Did you know that light moves faster than anything else in the world?

Some say that the greatest scientist who ever lived was a physicist. He was Isaac Newton, an Englishman who lived over three hundred years ago. The story goes that young Isaac became fascinated with what makes things move when he looked out his bedroom window and spied an apple falling from a tree in the yard. "Why do things fall down?" he asked himself. "Why don't they go sideways, or some other direction?" When he grew up he answered that question, and many others as well.

After a while, physicists learned the basic laws that described how large things like balls and planets move. They could predict exactly what the motions would be. What would physicists study next? In modern times, they began turning their attention from things that could be seen to things that were too small to see. They studied bits of matter called atoms, and then particles even smaller than atoms. The age of modern physics had begun.

Here's a picture of Isaac Newton thinking about why apples fall down.

Physicists study how things move—from the activities of the atom to the orbits of planets. (Pluto is usually the outermost planet, but until 1999 Neptune is orbiting outside Pluto's orbit.)

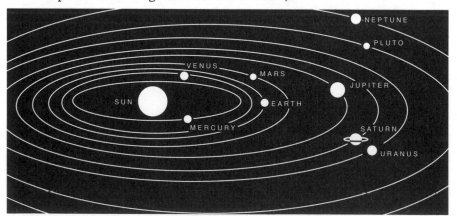

What Do Physicists Do Today?

What do physicists do today? A list would more than fill the pages of this book, so we'll just give two examples.

1) Physicists build and study lasers, which are devices that produce narrow beams of light. The light is all of one color, and can be so strong that these lasers can be used to drill holes through metal. Also, laser beams can be so narrow and delicate that they can be used to perform surgery on the eye.

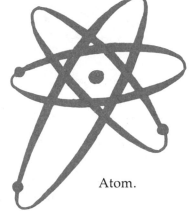

Atom.

2) Physicists study particles that are thousands of times smaller than the atom. The particles have strange names like leptons and hadrons. Will physicists discover even smaller particles?

Making Things: Engineering

Engineers build machines and bridges and buildings. Over four thousand years ago, the engineers of Egypt were asked to design huge pyramids for their rulers. Engineers planned and directed the construction of these mighty structures. Some of them were almost five hundred feet tall. They can still be seen along the banks of the Nile River in Egypt.

What kinds of work do engineers do today? Some, called civil engineers, are builders just like the Egyptians. They plan bridges, highways, and buildings.

Aeronautical engineers design many kinds of airplanes from giant jets to helicopters.

Chemical engineers design the factories that make materials like plastics.

Electrical engineers design power plants so that factories and homes will have plenty of energy. They build communications systems so powerful that astronauts thousands of miles from home can talk to people on earth.

Mechanical engineers help build machines called robots, which do jobs in places that are much too dangerous for people to go to—taking pictures of the very deepest parts of the oceans, for example.

Biomedical engineers make artificial limbs for people who have lost a leg or an arm. They design machines to clean the blood of people whose kidneys don't work properly.

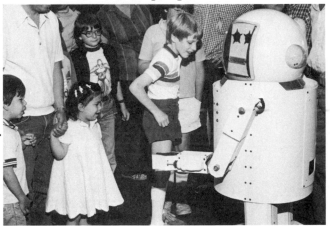

Denby the Robot walks, talks, turns his head, and shakes hands.

Those are just a few of the things engineers do. Can you think of other things they do? Have you ever built a machine or a building of blocks? Or made a doll, or a paper airplane? If so, you were being an engineer.

Our Own Planet: Study of the Earth

Geology is the name for the study of the earth—its violent interior, its surface, its oceans, and its continents. The prefix geo- comes from a Greek word meaning earth. People who study geology are called geologists.

From far away the earth looks calm. Photos taken from outer space make our planet earth seem a quiet place. But beneath the surface, where cameras cannot go, there is constant activity.

What goes on there inside the earth? The author J. R. R. Tolkien wrote books about imaginary creatures, called hobbits, who live below the earth's surface in a world called Middle Earth. These stories are wonderful fantasies, but really, the earth's interior is much too hot and turbulent for living things to call home.

The interior of the earth is made of hot melted rock containing so much energy that it sometimes bursts up through holes in the surface. These are volcanoes. Geologists study them very carefully. In May 1980, a volcano named Mount St. Helens erupted in the state of Washington. Geologists knew the eruption was coming. For several weeks beforehand they warned people to get out of the way, and they did—fast. Many lives were saved because of the geologists' warnings.

Mount St. Helens, the volcano, erupting.

Sometimes the energy inside the earth causes underground layers of rock to shift their position. This shifting inside the earth can be violent and cause the surface of the earth to shake, too. These events are called earthquakes. They can destroy buildings and bridges. Geologists are trying to learn how to predict when and where earthquakes will occur.

Look what the 1989 San Francisco earthquake did to this building.

Some geologists study the large masses of ice at the North and South Poles. Is the ice melting into the oceans, or is the ocean water freezing to make more ice? Will all the cities on the ocean coasts someday be under water from the melting ice?

Today, oil and gas from deep inside the earth supply most of the world's energy. Many geologists search for oil below the surface of the earth, so oil companies will know where to drill.

Geologists also study the age of our planet. They say that the earth is four and one half billion years old. How much is a billion? It's a thousand times as much as a million! So the earth is pretty old.

These are just a few of the things that geologists do.

Meteorology: Talking About the Weather

Suppose it's Thursday night. A farmer is wondering whether to plant his corn on Saturday. Will it rain, and make the soil too muddy to plant? Somewhere else, a family is discussing a picnic for Sunday. Will the skies be clear, or will they get wet? Both the farmer and the family will surely do one thing before making plans. They will listen to a weather report.

Meteorology is the science of weather. Meteorologists are the men and women who tell us how much snow fell in December and how warm it got yesterday. More important, they warn us when bad weather is headed our way. In September 1989, a small storm started forming over the Atlantic Ocean. For several days, meteorologists watched the storm grow and develop into a hurricane. They warned people living in the Virgin Islands and on the coasts of South Carolina and Georgia that the storm was about to hit. Even though Hurricane Hugo hurt some people and destroyed some buildings, the meteorologists' warnings saved many lives.

Not so long ago, people used sayings to help them predict the weather. The rhyme "Red sky at morning, sailor take warning, red sky at night, sailor's delight," told seamen when to expect bad weather or fair.

These days, meteorologists gather information in many ways. Balloons go very high in the sky with instruments to measure the temperature and the wind conditions. Weather satellites orbit the earth and send photos back to the ground. Radar locates rain clouds and thunderstorms. Special aircraft fly right into the eyes of hurricanes to measure their energy. Hundreds of weather stations across the United States measure temperature, wind speed, and precipitation. Huge computers collect all this information and help your local meteorologist—perhaps the TV weather person—make a forecast. Even with all this data, it is still impossible to predict the weather more than four or five days in advance.

The Sky Around Us: Astronomy

Today the world looks a lot different from the way it did in the days of our ancestors. Look around. What do you see? Books and blackboards, streets and automobiles. Maybe a computer. Imagine what our ancestors would say if they could see the world today. Imagine their surprise at all the changes.

But when we gaze into the sky, day or night, we see what people have seen for thousands of years—the sun, the moon, and the stars. They asked the same questions we do. How many stars are in the sky? How big is the universe?

Astronomy, the study of the universe beyond the earth, may be the oldest science. Ancient people noticed that in the spring the sun rises and sets at a different place in the sky from where it does in the fall. This fact helped farmers make a simple calendar to tell them when to plant and harvest their crops.

The stars helped travelers find their way. Many hundreds of years ago,

sailors made their way around the Pacific Ocean by looking at the night sky. They noticed that certain stars passed over the same island night after night. They could steer their vessels by the stars that would lead them to their destination.

This is a cloudlike star formation called the nebula Horsehead. Can you guess why it was named that?

As time went on, astronomers began to ask questions. Do the stars travel through space? Are there mountain ranges on the moon? To find the answers, men built instruments called telescopes to help them see into the sky.

Today is an exciting time for astronomers and for the rest of us, too. We no longer have to wonder about the moon—men have visited its surface.

In 1977, the Voyager 1 and Voyager 2 spacecraft were launched. Because the Voyagers will never return to earth, astronauts do not pilot them. The Voyagers have taken pictures of the earth, the moon, and other bodies—called planets—that revolve around the sun. But the best photographs will come in the future from telescopes we are beginning to send into space. They will take pictures of the moon and stars that are much better than those taken by earth telescopes. As astronomers study these pictures, they will be looking for answers to the question, how did our universe begin?

Simple Tools

Tools are things that help us accomplish some task. Although they don't do the work for us, they make the work easier for us to do. Here are some of the most important tools.

The Inclined Plane

The inclined plane is an example of a tool that doesn't look like a tool at all. The word "inclined" means leaning, and a plane is a flat surface. So an inclined plane is a leaning flat surface.

When Jack and Jill went up the hill to fetch a pail of water, they used an inclined plane. Their goal was to go from the bottom of the hill to the top. The distance from bottom to top was much too far to travel with one big jump, so they walked. Think how hard it would have been for them if they had to go up a high, up-and-down wall instead of a leaning surface. The inclined plane— the hill—let them spread out the work needed to get from bottom to top one step at a time.

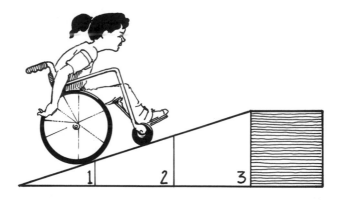

Wheels roll on inclined planes more easily than on stairs, so ramps are built to help people in wheelchairs travel more easily. These ramps make it possible for a wheelchair to roll off a sidewalk, across the street, then up onto the sidewalk on the other side.

Wedges

Wedges are "V"-shaped pieces of metal or wood. Some metal wedges are used to split logs. The tip of the "V" is placed on the end of the log, and a mallet is used to strike the flat end of the wedge. The wedge is hammered into the wood until it splits the log apart.

A look at the picture shows something neat about the way a wedge works. The man hammers from the top, but the wood is split apart from side to side. Can you figure out why?

Other examples of wedges are knives and nails.

Pegs, Nails, and Screws

We often need to put things together. Two pieces of paper can be joined with glue or staples or a paper clip. But when we want to attach heavy things we use pegs, nails, or screws.

Pegs are very strong. But they take some time to use because you have to drill holes for them to go into. So, nails are often used to hold pieces of wood together instead. Nails are made out of metal, which is harder than wood, and they have pointed ends, like a pencil, that you can hammer into wood without making a hole first. This means that things can be built more quickly with nails.

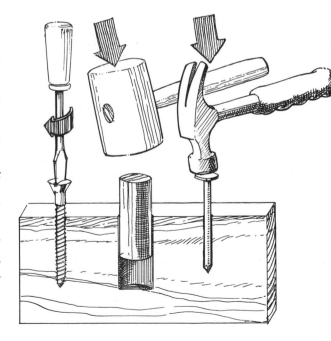

Pieces of wood can be joined even more strongly by using screws. When a nail is hammered into wood, the hole it makes has smooth sides. The nail is easily removed. But when we put a screw into wood, the hole created is not smooth. As the screw twists, it cuts grooves into the wood. A screw is harder to pull out than a nail. Try it!

Pulley

Have you ever seen a tug-of-war? Two teams grab opposite ends of a rope. Each team tries to pull the other side across a mark on the ground. In a tug-of-war, we try to make our opponents move in the direction that we pull on the rope.

Now, what about lifting a piano with a rope? Professional movers often use ropes to move pianos. Have you seen them? Do they pull in the direction they want the object on the other end of the rope to go, as the teams do in a tug-of-war? Not usually. They add a wheel or wheels to the ropes to make a pulley, and they pull down on the rope to make the piano go up. Let's see how that works.

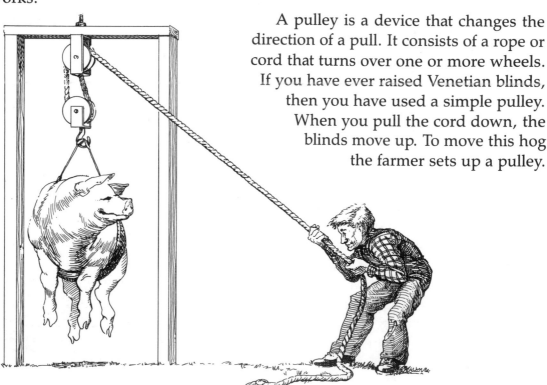

A pulley is a device that changes the direction of a pull. It consists of a rope or cord that turns over one or more wheels. If you have ever raised Venetian blinds, then you have used a simple pulley. When you pull the cord down, the blinds move up. To move this hog the farmer sets up a pulley.

First he attaches a wheel to the frame. Then he threads a rope from the top wheel around the bottom wheel and back over the top wheel. You can see this in this picture. He loops the ends of the sash that goes around the hog's middle over the hook on the lower wheel. Then he pulls on the loose end of the rope, and up goes the hog! The hog seems only half as heavy as it really is because the rope goes two feet for every foot the hog goes up. Would you rather use a pulley or your bare hands to lift a hog?

To find out more about pulleys, look them up in The Way Things Work, by David Macaulay, published by Houghton Mifflin Company, © 1988. Incidentally, this book is a fun source of information about all sorts of mechanical devices.

Iron and Steel

The first iron people used didn't have to be made in a fiery hot iron factory. It came right out of the sky.

Thousands of years ago, people looked up in the night sky to see a fantastic sight—fiery points of light streaking across the sky. These were shooting stars. Have you see them on a summer night? These shooting stars are not really stars at all. They are rocks from space called meteors. If we add an "ite" to the word meteor, we get meteorite. A meteorite is a meteor that falls through the sky and lands on the earth without burning up.

The ancients were so curious about the meteorites that they picked up these rocks that fell to earth. Inside the rocks they found a substance so special that they used it to make jewelry. As time passed, they learned to make tools and weapons from the material, which they called "the metal of heaven." Today we call this substance iron.

Before the discovery of iron, people made tools from wood and stone. But iron tools made farming much faster and easier. More people could be fed. Imagine digging up a whole garden with a stone or stick, and then think about how much easier it is to use a shovel with an iron blade. The discovery of iron was so important that we call the ancient time of its discovery the Iron Age.

This blacksmith is shaping a horseshoe. Can you tell if the horseshoe is hot?

The making and repairing of articles made of iron were important parts of pioneer life in our nation. Men called blacksmiths heated the iron to a red-hot glow in a type of fireplace called a forge. The hot iron was then hammered and bent into objects like horseshoes and hinges.

Iron is just as important today as it was in centuries past. These days, most iron comes in the form of iron ore found in the earth's crust. This ore is not pure iron, but a mixture of things. When the ore is placed in a very hot furnace, the iron melts and can be separated from its impurities. If the pure iron is then heated with carbon and oxygen, a very strong metal, called steel, is produced. Steel is very important to modern life. It is used to build automobiles and ships. It is needed to build buildings that are so tall they're called skyscrapers.

Lodestones, Magnets, and Compasses

Soon after people first discovered iron, they found some very unusual pieces of iron ore. These pieces, called lodestones, attracted other pieces of iron.

A lodestone is a natural magnet. You probably use magnets to hold notes and pictures on the steel door of your refrigerator. (Remember, the steel in a refrigerator is made from iron!) Two wooden spoons won't stick when brought close together, but see how a magnet clings to an iron frying pan!

Magnets can be very useful. One thing we can do with a magnet is make a compass. A compass consists of a tiny magnet in the shape of an arrow. This little arrow is set on a sharp point, so it can spin around. When it stops spinning, one end of the pin always points north. Hikers, campers, and explorers use the compass to help them find their way in unknown areas.

Finding Your Way With a Compass

Every year people get lost in the wilderness, sometimes for days or weeks. Suppose you and your friends got lost hiking in the country, and you couldn't see the city or even a road. Would you be able to find your way home? You could if you knew the right direction to the road.

You can be confident of finding your way if you have done two things: you know the right direction for home, *and* you brought a compass with you. With a compass it's easy to go in any direction, because the compass needle always points north. Take a look at a compass. Notice that when you turn it around, the needle always keeps pointing the same way—north.

Let's suppose you have to go *east* to find the road home. How would you use the compass to do it? To find out, let's practice. First, let's face in the direction of the needle. It always points north, so behind you must be south. Where is east? To the right or to the left? East is to your right, and west is to your left.

That's also the way maps work, remember? The top is north, the bottom is south, the right is east, the left is west. You can remember this idea by saying "Left-west, left-west." The words almost rhyme. Whenever you are looking north, west is always left.

Let's go back to where you are lost. Remember you have to go east to get to the road. East is to the *right* of where the needle points, so you can go east by

turning yourself until the needle is pointing to your *left*, and then you march straight ahead, always keeping the needle pointed to the left. Do you see why that will make you go east? From this example, you can figure out now how to go in any direction—by keeping the needle pointed to the correct place as you walk. Try it!

Finding Your Way Without a Compass

You can see why it's a good idea to take a compass on a hike. But suppose you don't have one, or you forgot it, or dropped it? Are you in trouble? Maybe, but not if you know a few things about nature.

When you are in the woods, take a look at the bottoms of some tree trunks. Do you notice that one side of the trunks has more green moss on it than the other sides? Moss likes to grow where the sun doesn't shine. In America, the sun never shines from the north. That's why moss likes to grow on the north side of American tree trunks. So, if you are in the woods, you can find north

by finding the moss on the trunks. Once you know where north is, you can go in the direction you want, just as with a compass.

Okay, you say, but suppose it's nighttime, and you can't *see* any moss. Have you got any ideas about how to go east to find the road? On a clear night you can find any direction—if you know how to find the North Star, Polaris. The easiest way to identify Polaris is to find the Big Dipper, and then use its pointing stars to find the North

Can you find Polaris by following the line made by the two stars in the front edge of the Big Dipper?

Star. All other stars change their position through the night, but Polaris never changes. It constantly points true north. Shakespeare once had a character say: "I am as constant as the northern star," which means that the person never changed.

If you practice direction finding, someday you may be glad you did.

Light

Try to imagine a world without light. Candles would stop burning, and lamps would go out. The stars wouldn't twinkle, and the moon wouldn't glow. Because the sun wouldn't shine, it would always be night. Everything would be black, and we could see nothing at all.

Our main source of light is the sun. At night, manmade sources of light, such as light bulbs and flashlights, help us see.

The speed of light is faster than anything else in the universe. Try aiming a flashlight at an object across a dark room. When you turn on the flashlight, the object seems to appear instantly. How long does it take light to get from the sun to the earth? The light that you see outdoors left the sun's surface eight minutes before you see it. Since the sun is 93 million miles away, you can imagine how fast it must travel to get to earth so soon—93 million miles in eight minutes!

When light strikes an object, several things can happen. If the object is transparent, like a windowpane, the light passes right through it, and things on the other side can be seen clearly. An object is said to be translucent when only part of the light passes through it, and things on the other side look like shadows. Your eyelids are translucent. When you close them on a bright sunny day, some light still reaches your eyes. When no light passes through it at all, an object is said to be opaque.

Have you ever seen your image in a spoon, or on the hood of an automobile or some other smooth surface? The light bounces from you to the surface, and the surface is so smooth that you can see yourself when the light bounces back to your eyes. A mirror is a smooth surface of glass with a silvery coating on the back. Light passes right through the transparent glass. It strikes the smooth silvery coating. The silver coating reflects the light, which passes back through the glass to your eyes. So you see your own reflection.

The glass in this window is transparent; the light passes through it.

The shade over this window is not transparent; it's translucent. Only some of the light that hits it gets through into the room.

STORIES OF SCIENTISTS

Galileo Galilei

In the sixteenth century a young Italian professor of mathematics named Galileo Galilei became interested in the study of the stars and planets. People still believed, and the Church still taught, that the sun and the stars circled around the earth. This belief made people feel powerful: if God created humans and placed them at the center of the universe, didn't that mean that man was the most important creature of all?

Galileo read an old, almost forgotten book by the astronomer Nicolaus Copernicus. It said that the earth was rotating and not the sun and stars. Galileo hoped he could use observations and math to *prove* what Copernicus had only guessed. To make his observations, Galileo designed an improved telescope. When he looked through it, objects looked bigger and closer than

Galileo presenting his invention, the telescope.

they seemed with his eyes. When Galileo turned his powerful instrument to the skies, he made three important discoveries.

He saw that the surface of the moon was not as perfect as everyone believed, but was marked with mountains, valleys, and craters. Second, the Milky Way was not a band of light, but clusters of stars—more than anyone could possibly count. Finally, one January night, Galileo looked at the planet Jupiter and saw three moons: two to the right of the big planet and one to the left of it. The next night, all three moons were to the left of Jupiter! What did that mean? Galileo concluded that the moons must be circling around the planet. And if that was true, then, not *every* object in the sky was circling around the earth!

Although Galileo's discoveries went against what the Church taught, his faith in God was strong. Galileo wanted to separate science from religion, to make everyone free to discuss ideas. Unfortunately, certain powerful people in the Church were frightened by free discussion. They placed Copernicus's writing on a list of forbidden literature, and ordered Galileo to stop defending his ideas about the earth moving.

But Galileo just couldn't control his excitement, or deny what he believed was true. He wrote a dialogue containing his ideas. A dialogue is a kind of writing in which two (or more) people discuss and argue about ideas. Many ancient writers used dialogues to present their theories—never revealing which speakers in the dialogue they agreed with. Sixteen years after Galileo was forbidden to say either that the earth moved or that it was not the center of the universe, he published *A Dialogue Concerning the Two Chief World Systems*.

It got him in trouble. One person in the dialogue was stubbornly old-fashioned, and said that the sun and the stars did circle the earth, just as the Church taught. Another said that the earth rotated around its own axis, thus making the sun and stars *seem* to circle the earth. A third person was open-minded about the two theories.

The dialogue did not fool the Church authorities. They understood that Galileo had gone against the Church's orders, and had not kept silent about his views. Soon he paid a high price for disobeying the Church. He was held a prisoner in his own home and forced to swear in writing that he believed earth sat still at the center of the universe. Old, sick, and humiliated, Galileo signed the hated document. But no one could silence his thoughts or change the truth. According to legend, as Galileo slowly rose from his knees, he softly said under his breath, "But it *does* move."

Thomas Edison

Have you ever turned on a light bulb? Or gone to the movies? Or listened to recorded music? If so, then you have benefited from the imagination and creativity of one man: Thomas Edison. "Genius is 1 percent inspiration and 99 percent perspiration," Edison said, and his lifetime accomplishments proved him right.

Born the last of seven children, Thomas Edison attended school for a total of only three months! Although his mother continued to teach him at home for several years, most of his knowledge came from books. Edison went deaf at age twelve, and this misfortune launched him on a program of reading and making scientific experiments. His boyhood job was selling candy, food, and newspapers on a railroad, so he would often set up traveling laboratories in the baggage car, where he carried out his experiments.

Thomas Edison.

Later, as a young man, Edison worked as a telegraph operator, and soon invented a device that automatically repeated Morse Code messages. After that, he had several other new ideas. But his 1869 improvement of a ticker-tape machine established him as a "real" inventor. He received a forty-thousand-dollar prize for this innovation, and he used the money to set up a private, fifty-man laboratory. This was the first modern research laboratory because researchers worked in teams to investigate problems systematically.

Thomas Edison was very practical. He would notice a need and invent something to fill it. Did he just dream up solutions out of thin air? To the public, it seemed that he did. But in reality, he invented by trial and error. After reading everything written about a topic, Edison would test hundreds—even thousands—of possibilities. After failing eight thousand times to make a storage battery, Edison remarked, "Well, at least we know eight thousand things don't work." He always wanted to avoid duplicating mistakes, so he recorded his blunders as well as his hunches, ideas, and procedures in a series of notebooks.

At one time, Edison was the best-known American in the world, with 1,093 patents issued in his name. His laboratory produced electric generators and locomotives and set the stage for future developments in modern surgery, television, radio broadcasting, and electronic musical instruments. But Edison is best known for:

The *phonograph,* which recorded and replayed music or human voices. (The first words spoken into the phonograph recorder were, "Mary had a little lamb.")

An *incandescent light,* which produced steady, bright light by heating a filament of conducting material with electricity. This creation was the product of 9,990 separate experiments. Edison's incandescent light was soon improved by the use of a long-lasting filament invented by the African-American scientist Lewis Latimer.

Motion pictures—The first "movies" were a series of photographs taken at the rate of sixteen per second. When the strips of film were pulled across a projector light, they reproduced a lifelike motion. It didn't take long for Edison to combine movies with his phonograph to create talking pictures.

Thomas Edison didn't carry a watch. Yet, to him, time was the most valuable thing in the world. He would work forty to fifty hours at a stretch, catching naps on a worktable. He proved that creativity is not easy; it takes long, hard work. If something didn't work the first time (or the second, or the hundredth), he simply kept trying until he succeeded.

Florence Nightingale

As the young daughter of wealthy British parents, Florence Nightingale faced a rosy future. It was expected that she would marry a rich gentleman and raise a large family. But Florence had different plans. She was an intelligent, independent young woman, full of desire for a career that would serve humankind.

When Florence Nightingale announced she wanted to work as a hospital nurse, her family was upset. Nevertheless, she traveled to Germany to train in a school orphanage and hospital. Returning to England, she became head of a nursing home in London. In time she turned it into a model institution that was open to patients of all classes and religions.

In October of 1854, Florence Nightingale led thirty-eight nurses to Turkey to care for British soldiers wounded in the Crimean War. She found terrible conditions in the British hospital. The buildings were infested with fleas and rats. They were built over open sewers that polluted the air and water. The wards were overcrowded and dirty, and the soldiers had little food. She soon discovered that more men died from disease than from their wounds.

Florence Nightingale.

She fought for improvements. Men in authority objected that she, a woman, was demanding changes. They wanted women to be quiet and meek. Also, nurses were something new in war, and the officers objected to having them near the soldiers. So Nightingale set rigid codes of dress, training, and behavior for her nurses. Her principles form the basis of the modern nursing profession.

By day, Florence Nightingale worked to improve the cleanliness of the hospital and brought in food and medical supplies. At night, she wandered miles of hospital corridors, caring for the injured and sick by the light of an oil lamp. Newspaper reporters found out what she was doing, and wrote about her. She became known as "The Lady of the Lamp." She became world famous for her work.

Upon her return to England, she used her great fame to reform medical care. She wrote reports to show that fewer people would die if hospitals were cleaner. Her reports, filled with facts and figures, proved her point, thus showing that important social problems could be analyzed by using numbers. People were persuaded by her facts and figures. By 1861, every one of her proposed reforms was in place.

She never fully recovered from a sickness she suffered during the war. Weak and frail, she became bedridden. But she did not stop working to help people. She helped start the Nightingale School for training nurses in London. She spoke out for the poor and underprivileged.

Florence Nightingale's life speaks strongly to us across the years: Think for yourself. Try to serve other people. People are different from one another, so don't be limited by what others expect of you. When faced with opposition, don't yell and scream. Support your opinions with facts. They make the best argument.

Mae Jemison

Imagine you're lying on your back, strapped into a chair, with your knees bent in front of you. You feel your heart pounding with excitement as you hear a voice on the earphones inside your helmet counting down slowly, "Three, two, one." Then, beneath you, a deep rumble starts as rocket fuel ignites in the huge engines. You feel a lurch as the docking mechanisms let go, and your rocket begins to rise. Lift-off!

This is the moment Mae Jemison has been waiting and working for since 1987. The first African-American female astronaut-in-training at the National Aeronautics and Space Administration (NASA), Jemison is scheduled to "fly" in September 1992. She is to serve as a specialist on Spacelab-J, a joint Japanese-American research project.

Mae Jemison was thirty-three when she was selected for NASA's astronaut training program. Astronaut candidates must have science degrees. They must be fit and healthy with normal blood pressure and good eyesight. They must stand between five feet and six feet four inches tall. They must complete a one-year training program that includes water-survival lessons and weightless walks in a huge antigravity tank.

Mae Jemison.

Since completing the training program, Mae Jemison has had several job assignments. She helped prepare the space shuttle for launch and countdown by checking the satellite that is piggybacked on the shuttle. She checked the heat-protection tiles that allow the shuttle to come back to earth without burning up. She worked in a NASA laboratory to ensure that the shuttle computer software was operating correctly.

On the 1991 mission, astronaut Jemison says that her "responsibilities are to be familiar with the shuttle and how it operates, to do the experiments once you get into orbit, to help launch the payloads or satellites, and also to do extra-vehicular activities, or space walks."

How did Mae grow up to become such a special person? Science—especially astronomy—fascinated her from childhood.

She also had a strong desire to help other people. Born in Alabama, but raised in Chicago, she studied chemical engineering and African-American culture and history at Stanford University. To help others, she decided to become a doctor. While still a medical student, she went to Cuba and Kenya on study trips, then worked in a refugee camp in Thailand. She spent three years in West Africa as a doctor with the Peace Corps. When Dr. Jemison finally returned to the United States, she settled in California to practice medicine. And it was then that she decided to reach for the stars.

Mae Jemison's first application to NASA was not successful. Then, in 1986, the *Challenger* space shuttle exploded, killing all aboard. NASA did not recruit any new astronauts for about a year. When it finally reopened its application process, Mae Jemison was ready, and so was NASA. After being selected as a minority astronaut, Mae Jemison received a good deal of attention from newspapers and television. She explained to reporters that the space program and other fields in high technology offer promising careers for African-Americans and other minorities who study hard and make the most of their opportunities.

Illustration and Photo Credits

Artists Rights Society, N.Y. Copyright 1991/ADAGP: 170

The Bettmann Archive:
53(a,b), 56, 95(a,b), 97, 108, 109, 110(b,c), 111, 113(b), 114, 115, 124, 135(a), 138, 141, 142(b), 143, 144, 146, 149, 151(a), 173, 174(a), 186(a,b), 272(b), 276, 284(a), 288, 296, 301, 305

British Library Board: 180

Chesterwood, a Museum Property for the National Trust.
Photographer: De Witt Ward: 182(a,b)

Padraic Colum, *The Golden Fleece and the Heroes Who Lived Before Achilles*, The MacMillan Company, 1921: 59(c), 60, 62(b), 105

Arthur Bernard Cook, *Zeus: A Study in Ancient Religion*, Volume 3, Part 1, Cambridge University Press, 1940: 55, 63(b)

The Thomas Gilcrease Museum: 130(b)

Max Hirmer, Munich: 53(c), 113(a)

Kunsthistorisches Museum: 179

Courtesy of the Library of Congress: 136, 140, 142(a), 145, 147, 150, 151(b), 303

The Louvre: 102

Massachusetts Division of Fisheries and Wildlife: 271(b), 273

Massachusetts Historical Society: 130(a), 131

Metropolitan Museum of Art, Harris Brisbane Dick Fund, 1964. (64.251): 122

Metropolitan Museum of Art/Gift of Henry G. Marquand, 1889: 184

Metropolitan Museum of Art/Purchase, 1890 Levi Hale Willard Bequest. (90.35.3): 175

Metropolitan Museum of Art/the Alfred Stieglitz Collection, 1949. (49.59.1): 178

Museo Nazionale Romano: 117

National Aeronautics and Space Administration: 307

National Gallery of Art, Washington, D.C., From the Collection of Dorothy Braude Edinburg/B-30503, SHELL, © 1928, Georgia O'Keeffe, 1887–1986: 172

Index